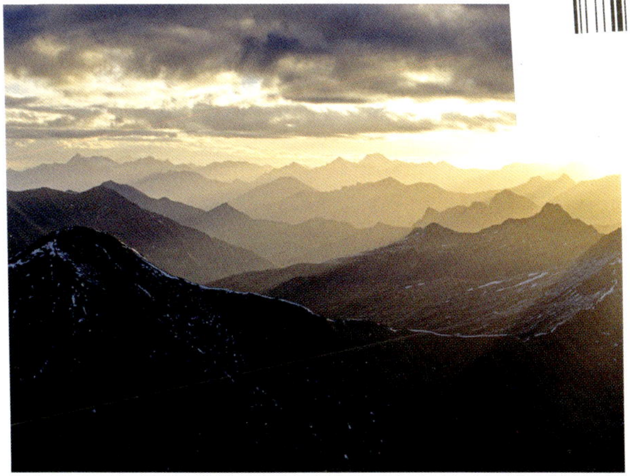

NATIONAL PARKS OF NEW ZEALAND

PHOTOGRAPHY BY ROB SUISTED
TEXT BY ALISON DENCH

NEW HOLLAND

CONTENTS

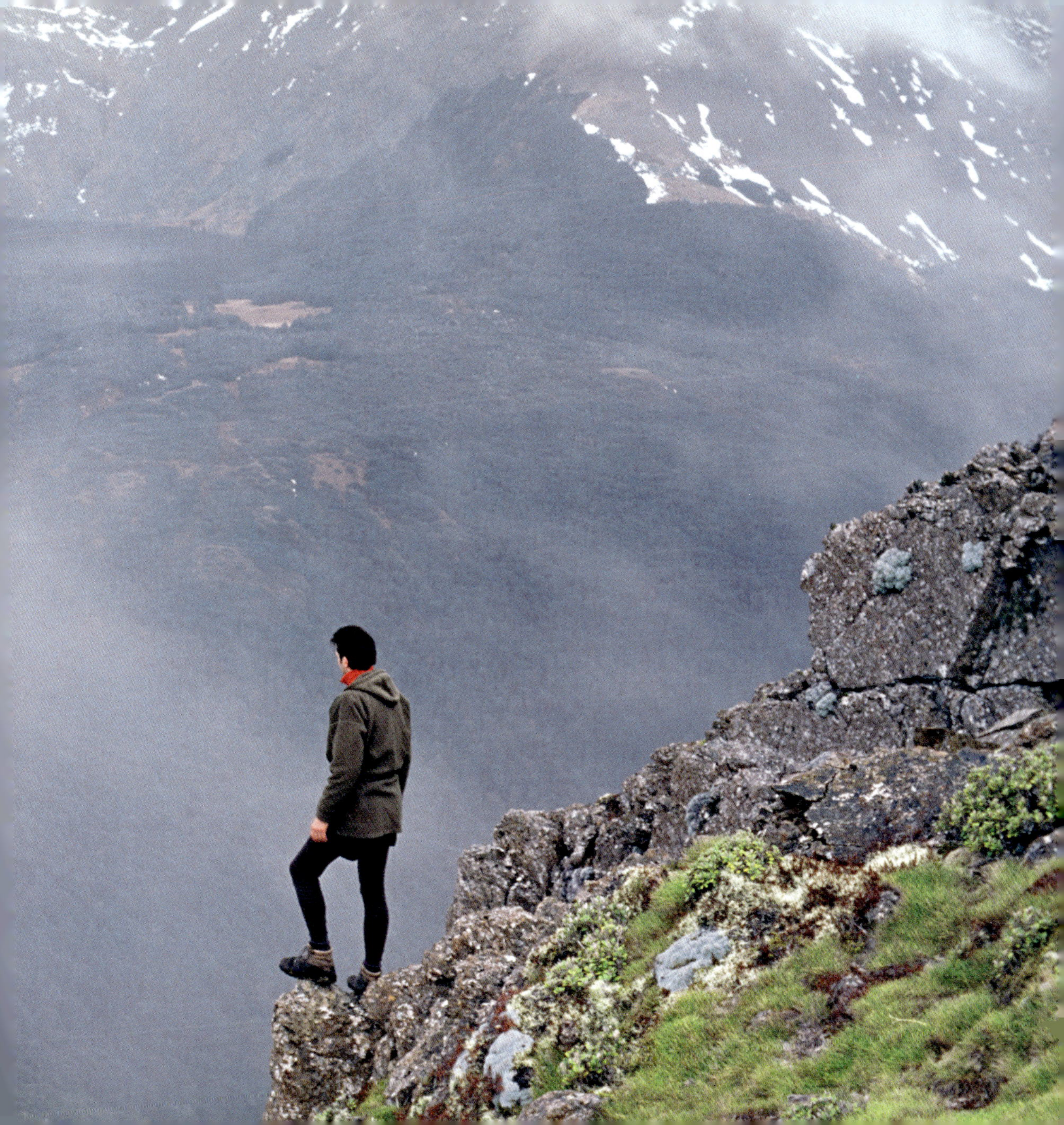

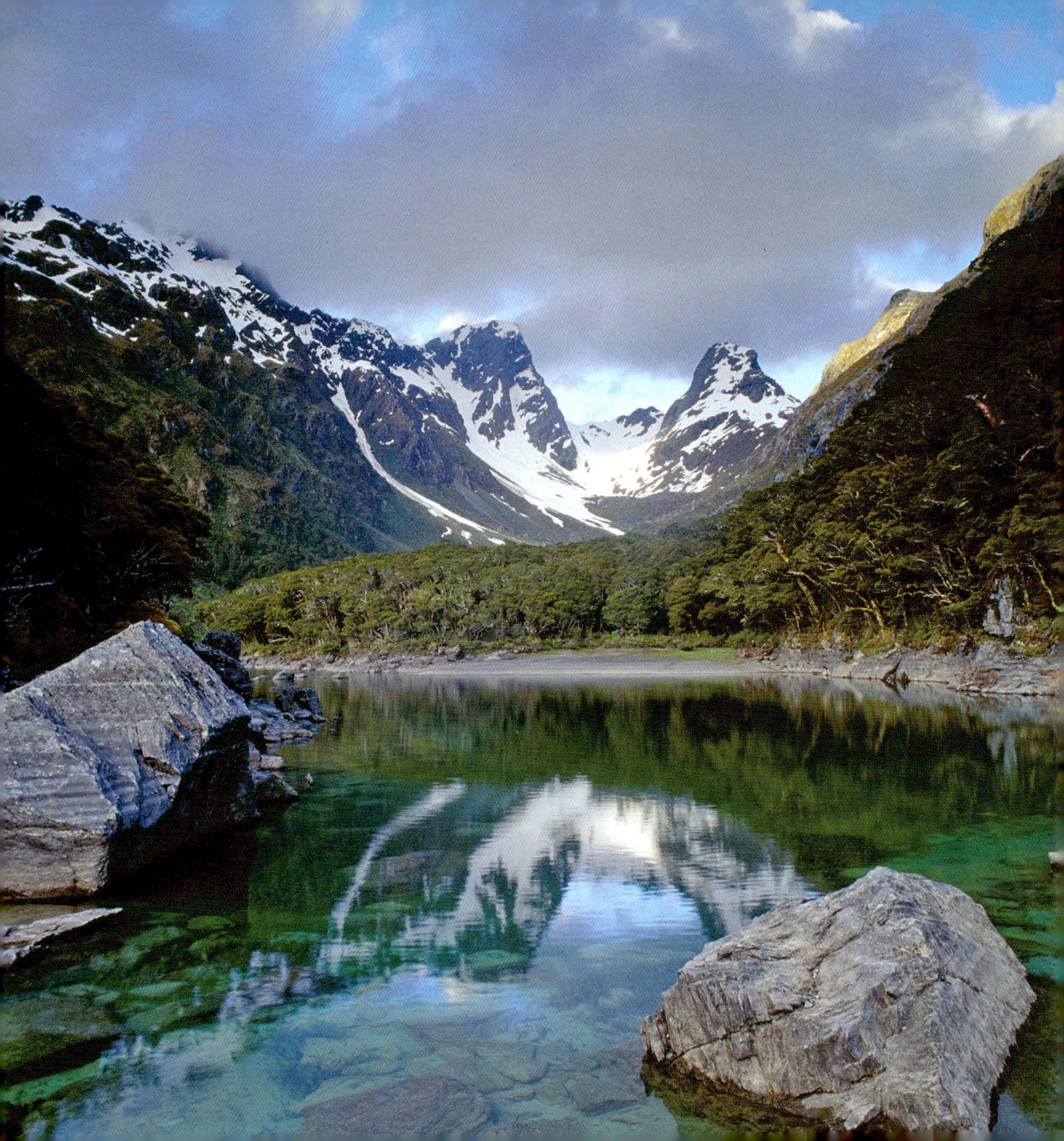

INTRODUCTION

New Zealand's national parks are the country's treasure houses. These wild areas, found in all three of the main islands, represent every kind of landscape from snowy mountain massifs to lush subtropical rainforests, from barren deserts to wetlands abundant in bird life, and from alpine meadows to golden beaches and wave-lashed rocky coasts. They offer vivid demonstrations of the power of natural forces and the way they have shaped both the land and lives of those who live and travel here.

Different people enjoy national parks in different ways. For some, the inspiring surroundings are the perfect setting to tune in to the environment and learn to respect it. If you take the time to listen, you will hear epic stories of geological upheaval, fascinating tales of the adaptability of wildlife and moving histories of human endeavour. For others the parks are adventure playgrounds in which to tackle physical challenges and test endurance. Some like to hunt or fish. For still others, they are a spiritual haven or a place of contemplation.

New Zealand's pioneering national park, Tongariro, was among the first in the world. Created in 1885 when Tuwharetoa chief Horonuku Te Heuheu Tukino IV made a gift to the nation of tribal land around the central North Island volcanoes, it was the starting point for a network of parks that over the following 120 years gradually built up to number 14. The parks are outstanding examples of landscapes and ecosystems, where visitors experience wild places on nature's terms and human interference is kept to a necessary minimum. They are run by the Department of Conservation, which manages access and is responsible for facilities such as trails, huts and campsites. The department must strike a balance between encouraging visitors and keeping the delicate ecosystems from harm.

There are many ways to move around the parks: by road, on foot on the extensive network of walking tracks, on skis in the mountains, or by kayak or canoe on the rivers and lakes. Commercial operators offer further options: bird-watching or historic tours, four-wheel-drive trips, cruises or scenic flights.

The national parks of New Zealand celebrate the beauty and diversity of these islands and they are a source of great pride for New Zealanders. Appropriately enough for a priceless resource, they are free for all to enter.

Left: Lake Mackenzie below Emily Pass and, to the right, Emily Peak. Fiordland National Park.

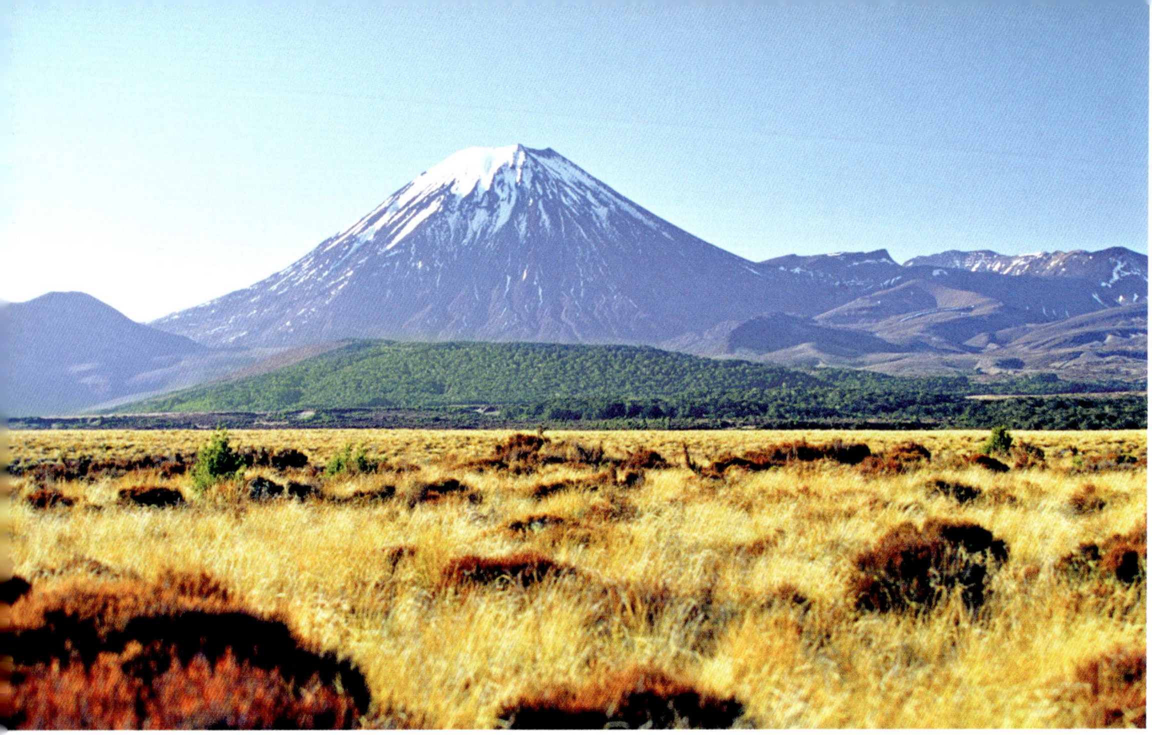

TONGARIRO

In New Zealand's first national park, created in 1885, three active volcanoes – Tongariro, Ngauruhoe and Ruapehu – rise suddenly above the plateau of the central North Island. There is volcanic ash underfoot, and hot mineral springs, steam vents and crater lakes are scattered among the rivers, lakes and waterfalls, providing an unforgettably incongruous setting for the familiar mountain pursuits of skiing, climbing and hiking. Forests grow at lower altitudes and alpine herbfields and glaciers at higher altitudes, and a unique desert area occupies the east. The park has been designated by UNESCO as a dual World Heritage Site, in recognition of both its Maori spiritual and cultural associations and its extraordinary volcanic features.

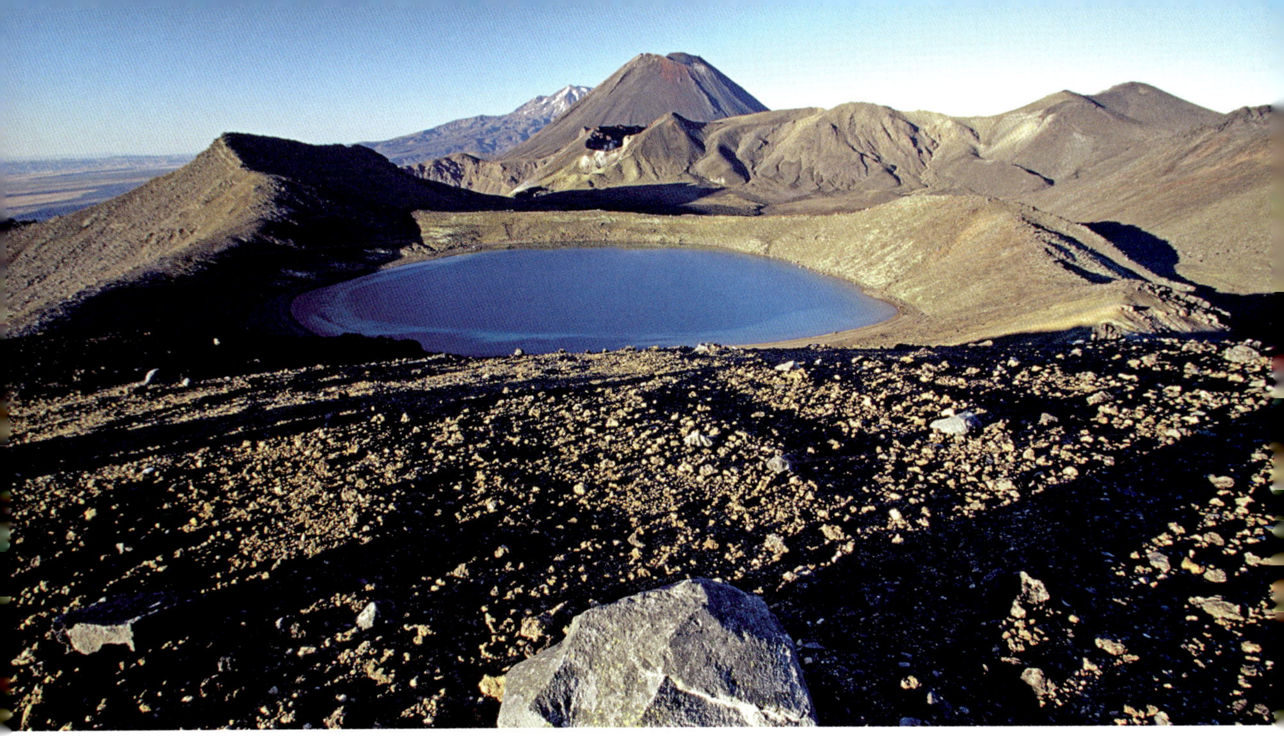

Left: Mt Ngauruhoe is one of New Zealand's several active volcanoes. It first erupted from the flank of Mt Tongariro about 2500 years ago.

Above: The popular Tongariro Alpine Crossing day walk passes by Blue Lake, a pool of acidic water in one of the volcanic craters that scar Mt Tongariro.

Right: The neo-Georgian Chateau Tongariro Hotel occupies a prime site on the slopes of Mt Ruapehu. Just up the road are the chairlifts of Whakapapa ski area.

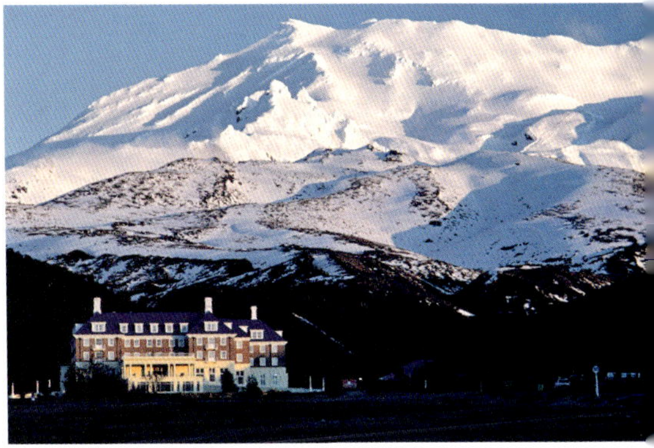

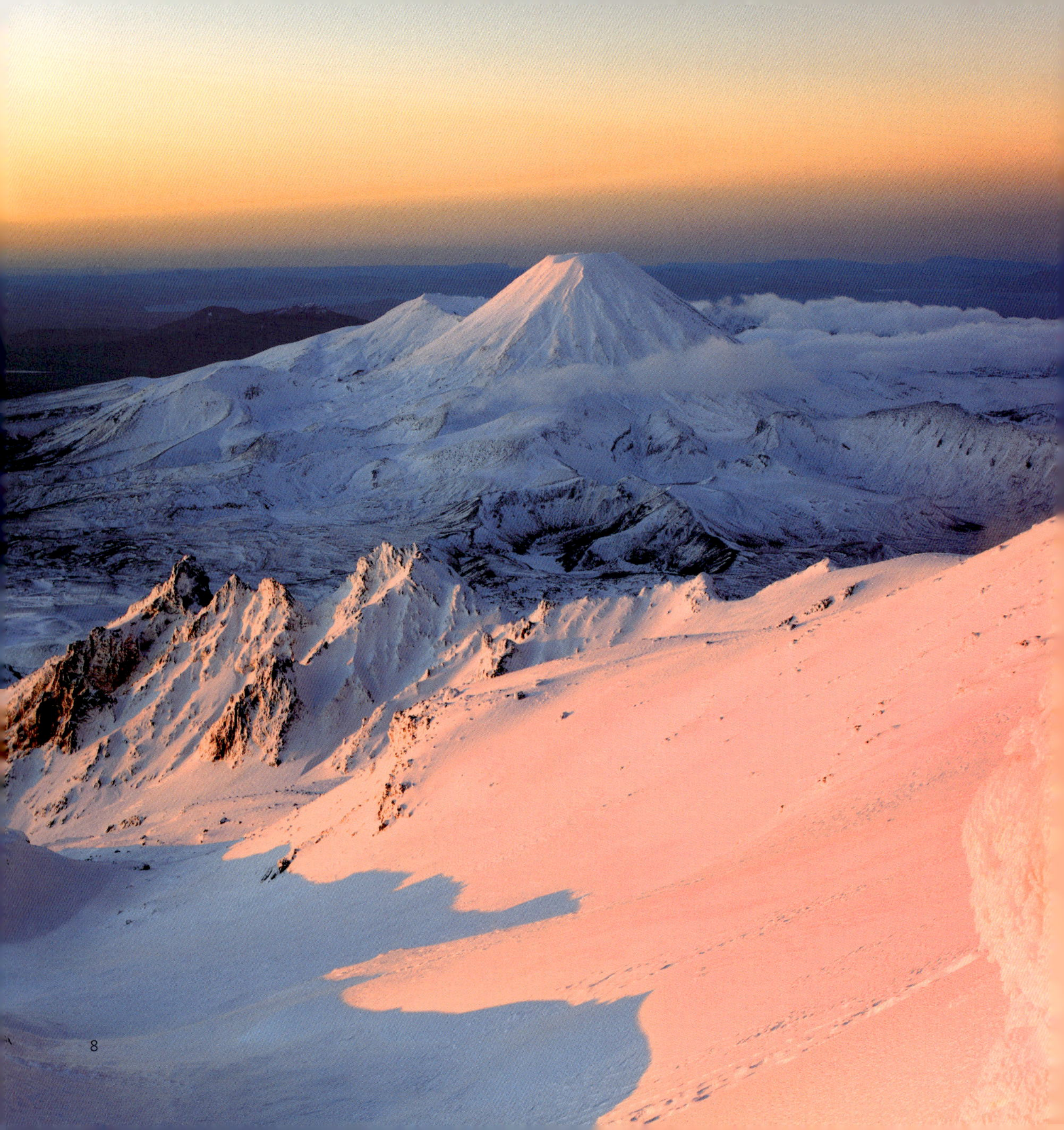

Left: Winter snow blankets the Pinnacle Ridge of Mt Ruapehu and, beyond, Mt Ngauruhoe. Sunset is a magical time in Tongariro National Park.

Right: A climber negotiates an icy ridge above the Summit Plateau of Mt Ruapehu. At 2797 m, Mt Ruapehu is the highest mountain in the North Island.

Below: Red tussock is one of the few plants that grow in the Rangipo Desert, a raw and forbidding place in the rain shadow of Mt Ruapehu.

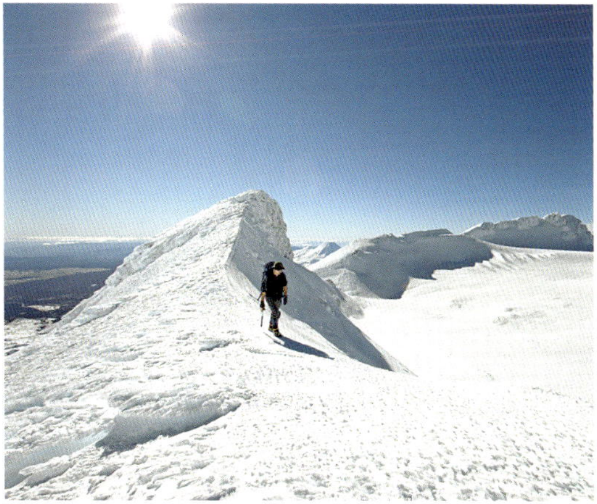

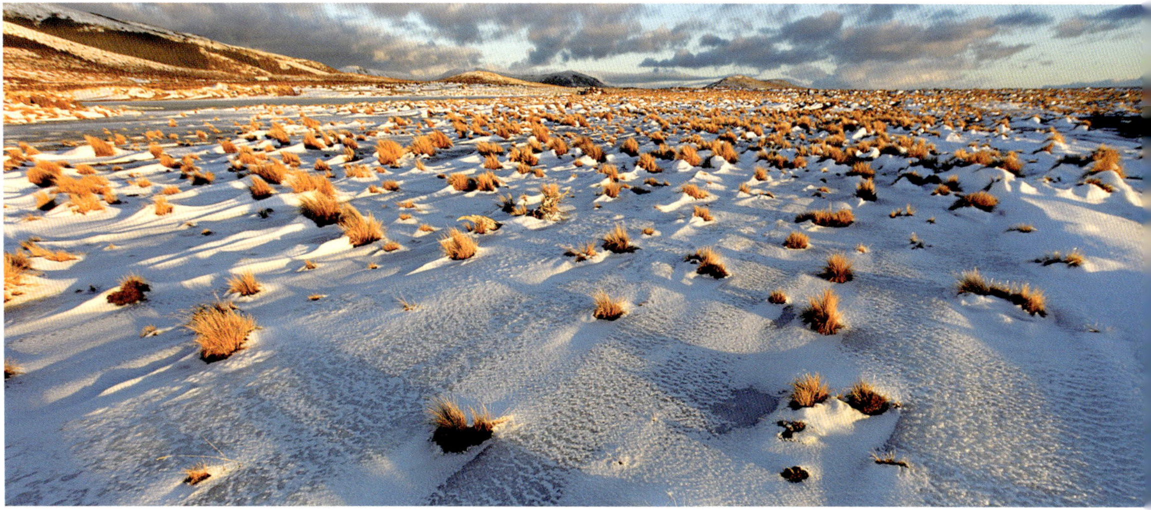

Right: The volcanic peaks of Ruapehu, Ngauruhoe and Tongariro create a dramatic backdrop to Lake Taupo.

Below: Snow covers the Mangatepopo Valley section of the Tongariro Alpine Crossing. During summer the track is a demanding day walk, but in winter it becomes a challenge for mountaineers.

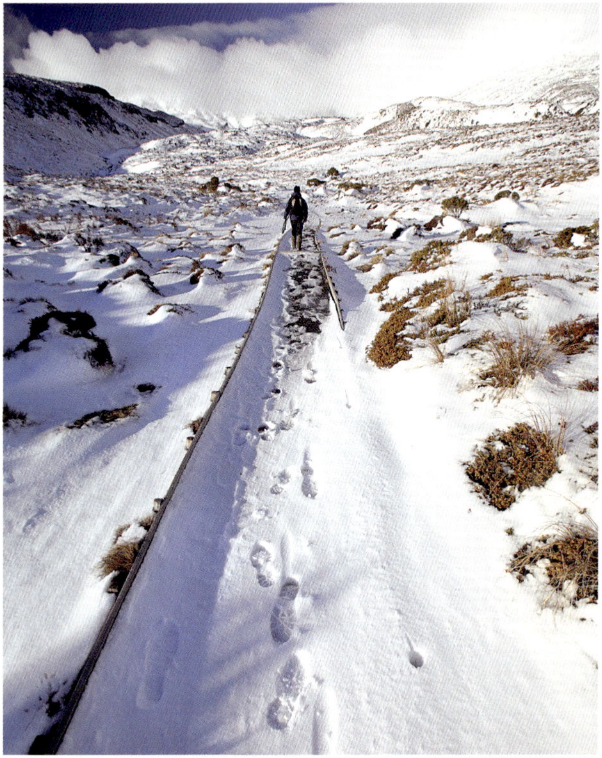

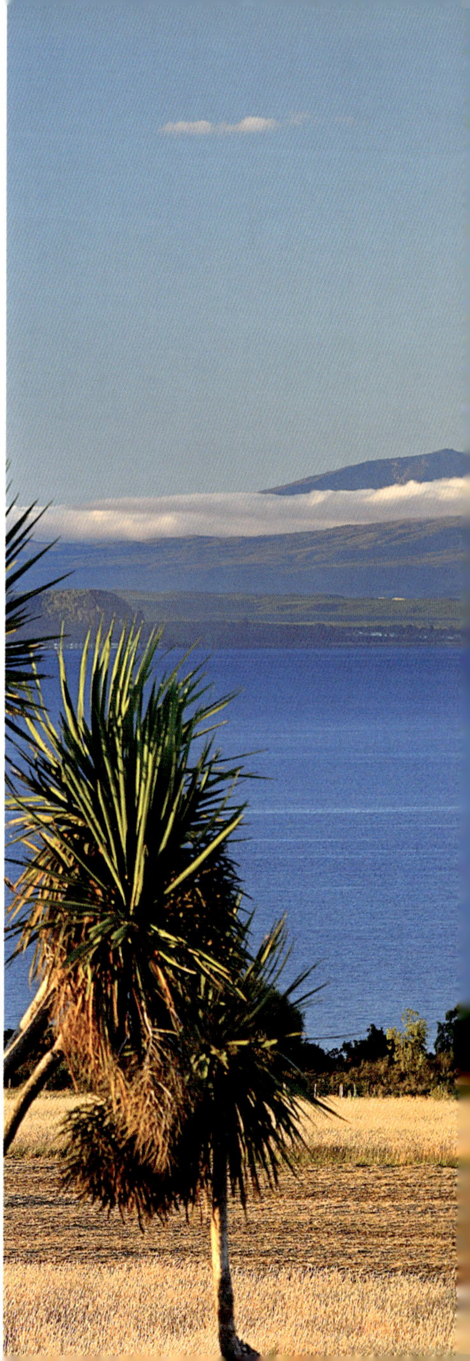

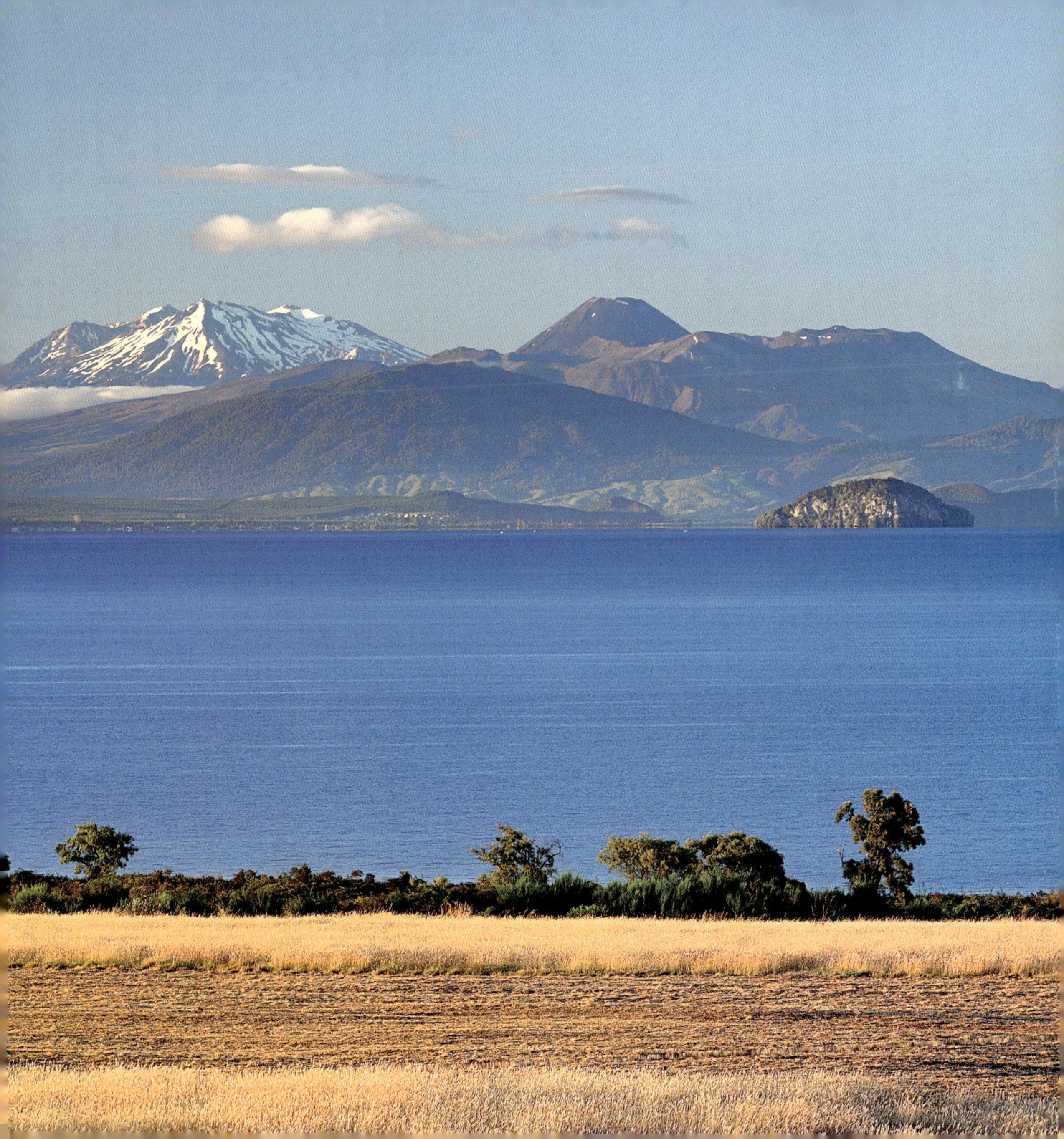

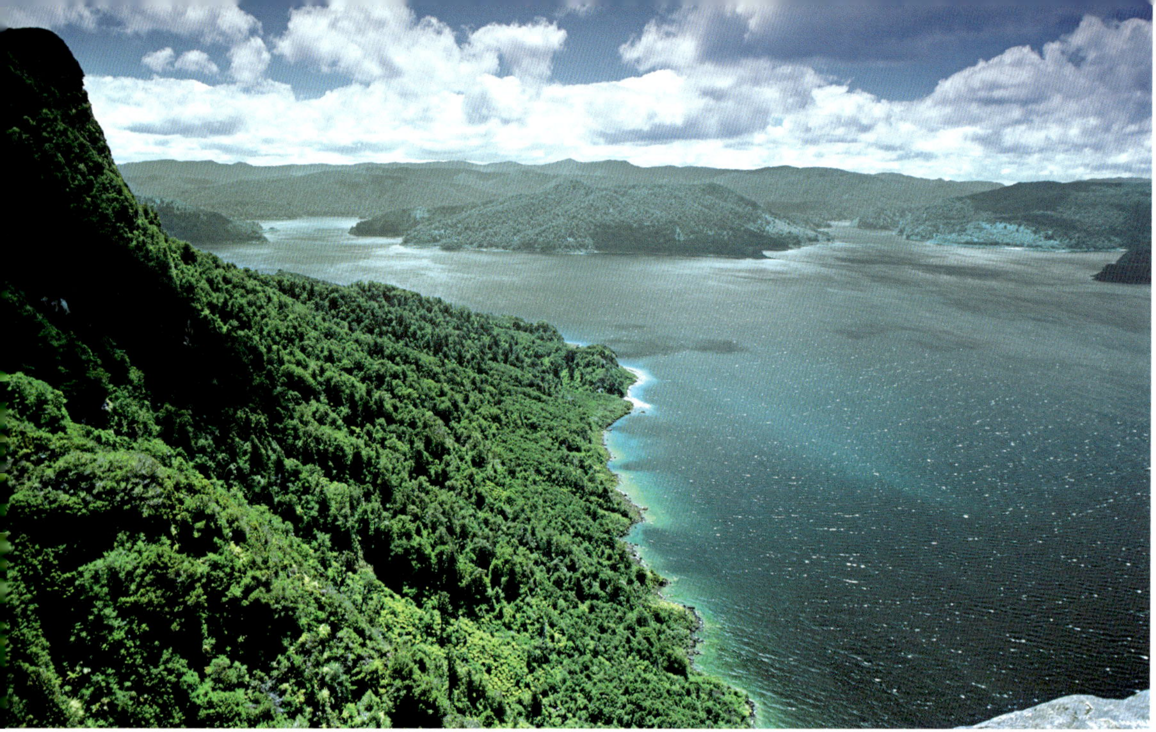

TE UREWERA

Te Urewera has for many centuries been home to the Tuhoe people, and the tribe's links with this remote rugged landscape are still powerful. Mist often shrouds the hills, a reminder that Ngai Tuhoe are descended from the mist maiden Hine-pukohu-rangi, and the park has many places that are sacred to the tribe. There is just one road, taking visitors to moody Lake Waikaremoana at the heart of the immense park, and from here the exploration must continue on foot or by boat. Te Urewera's inaccessibility has meant that a prodigious diversity of plant and bird life has been retained. Isolated ridges and valleys cloaked in untouched native forest provide the perfect habitat for almost the full complement of North Island native birds.

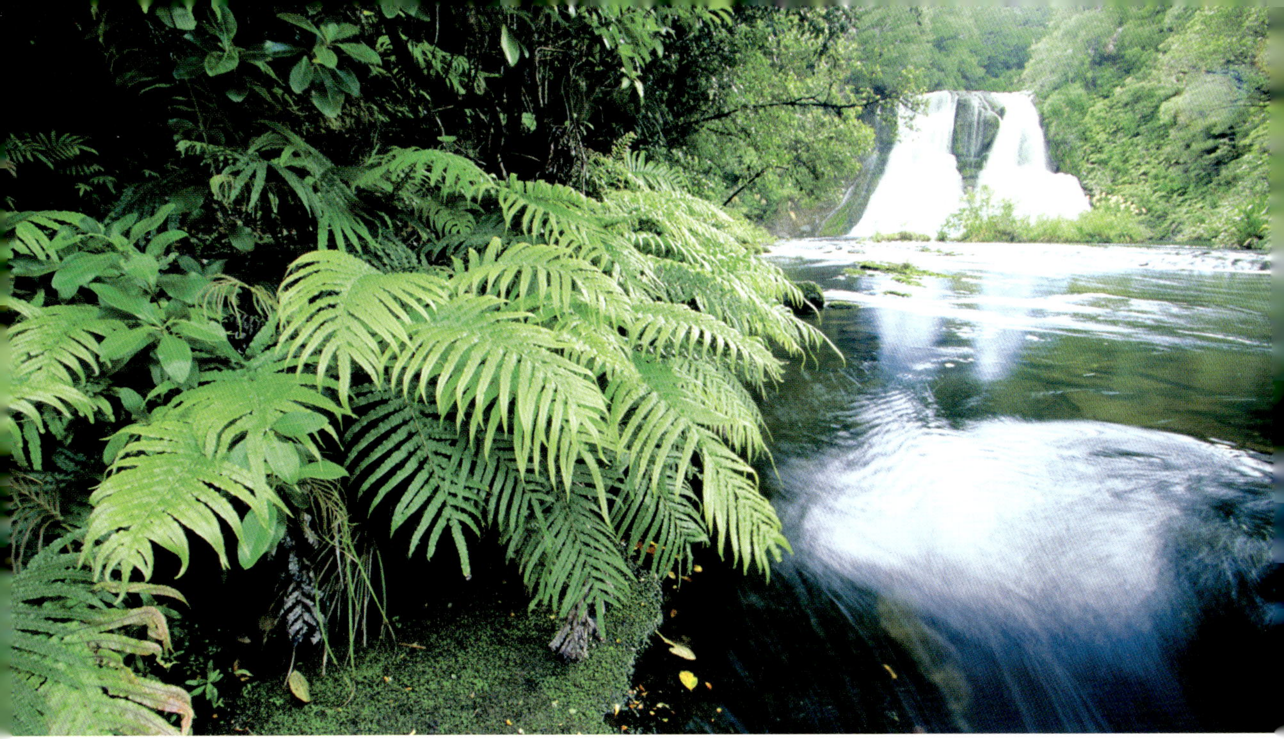

Left: Near Panekiri Bluff, hikers on the Lake Waikaremoana Great Walk are rewarded after a stiff uphill climb with views over the lake to the densely forested northern part of Te Urewera National Park.

Above: Aniwaniwa Stream tumbles 15 m over rocks at the Momahaki Falls before flowing on to nearby Lake Waikaremoana.

Right: The endangered whio/blue duck finds a refuge in the remote river valleys of Te Urewera National Park.

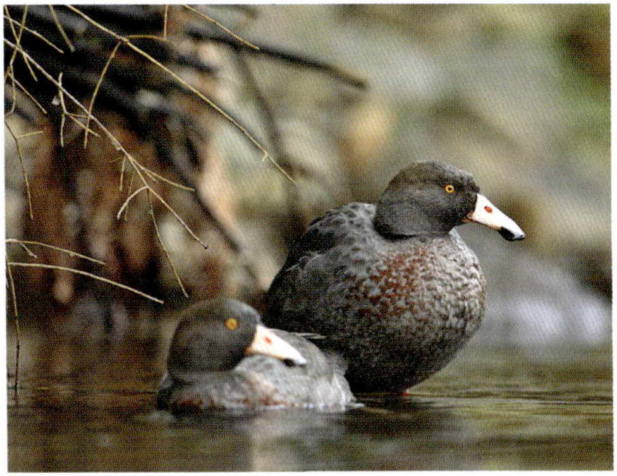

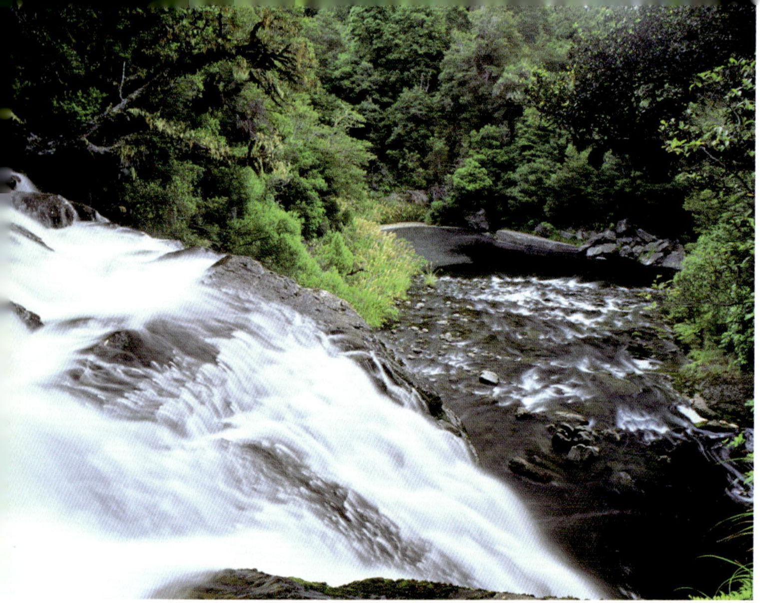

Left: Aniwaniwa Stream makes the leap from the top of Te Tangi-o-Hinerau. In Tuhoe legend, Hinerau was a beautiful woman whose tears formed the waterfall.

Below: Toetoe grasses, tree ferns and podocarp forest enclose Waiiti Stream in the northern part of the park.

Right: The Mokau Stream lives up to its Maori name, which means 'meandering', as it leaves the native forest to join Lake Waikaremoana.

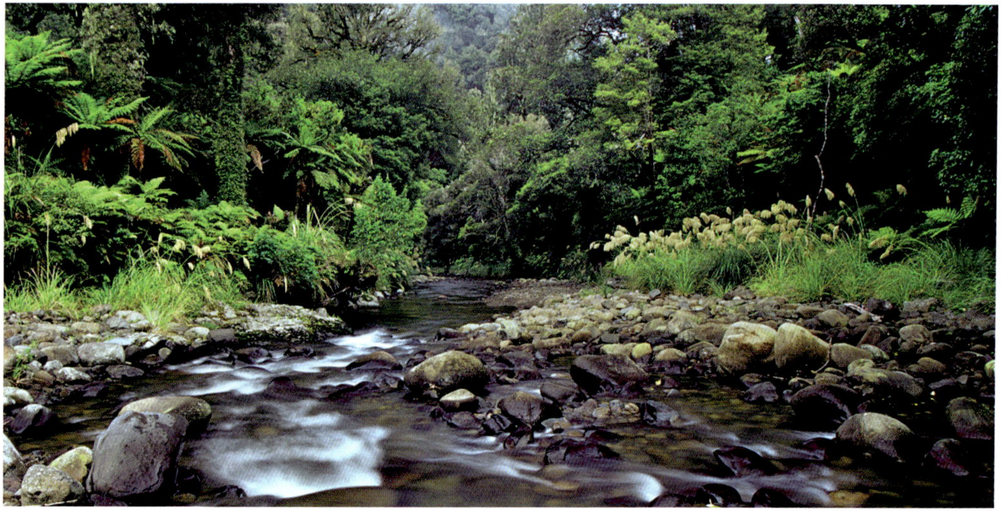

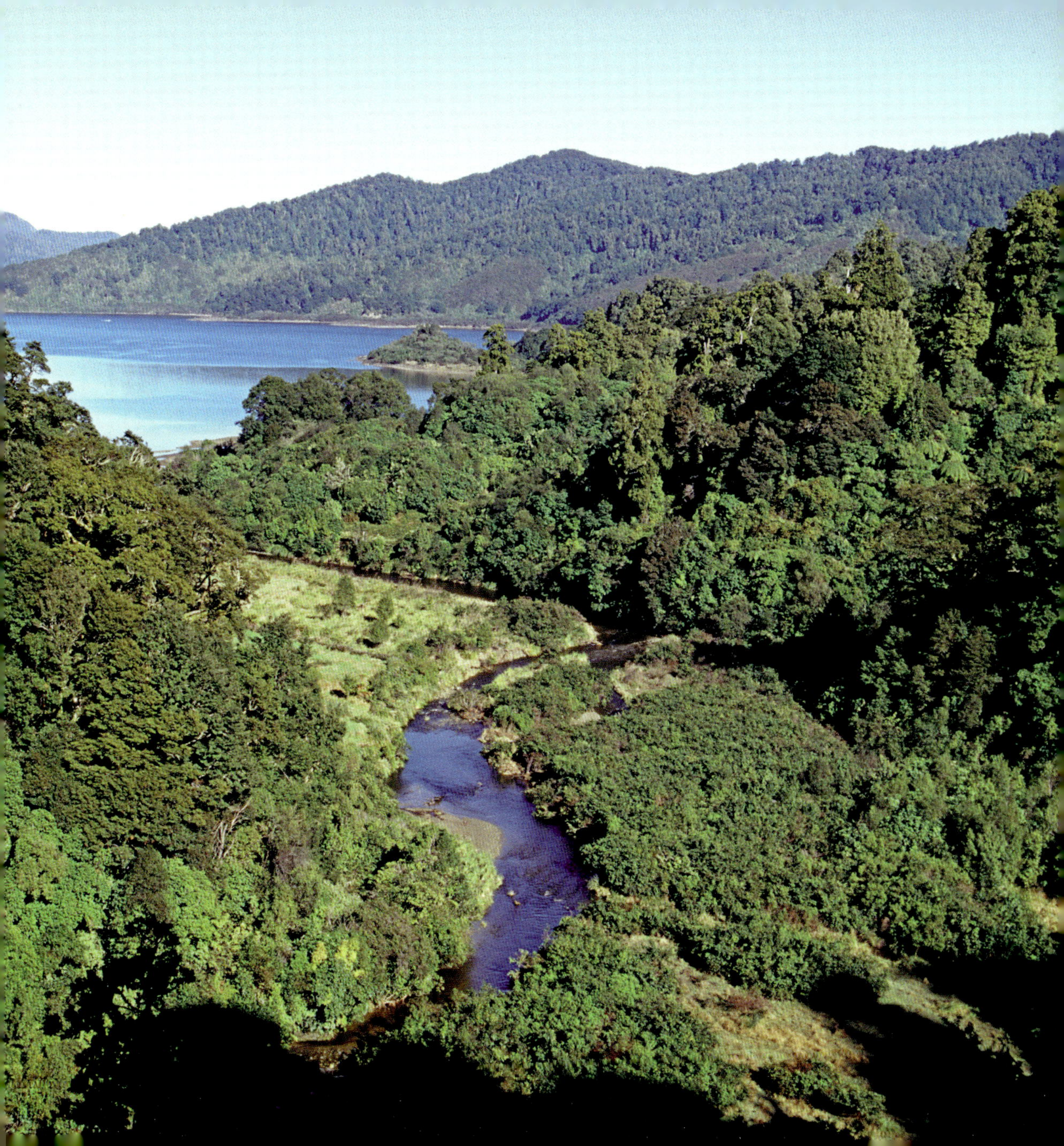

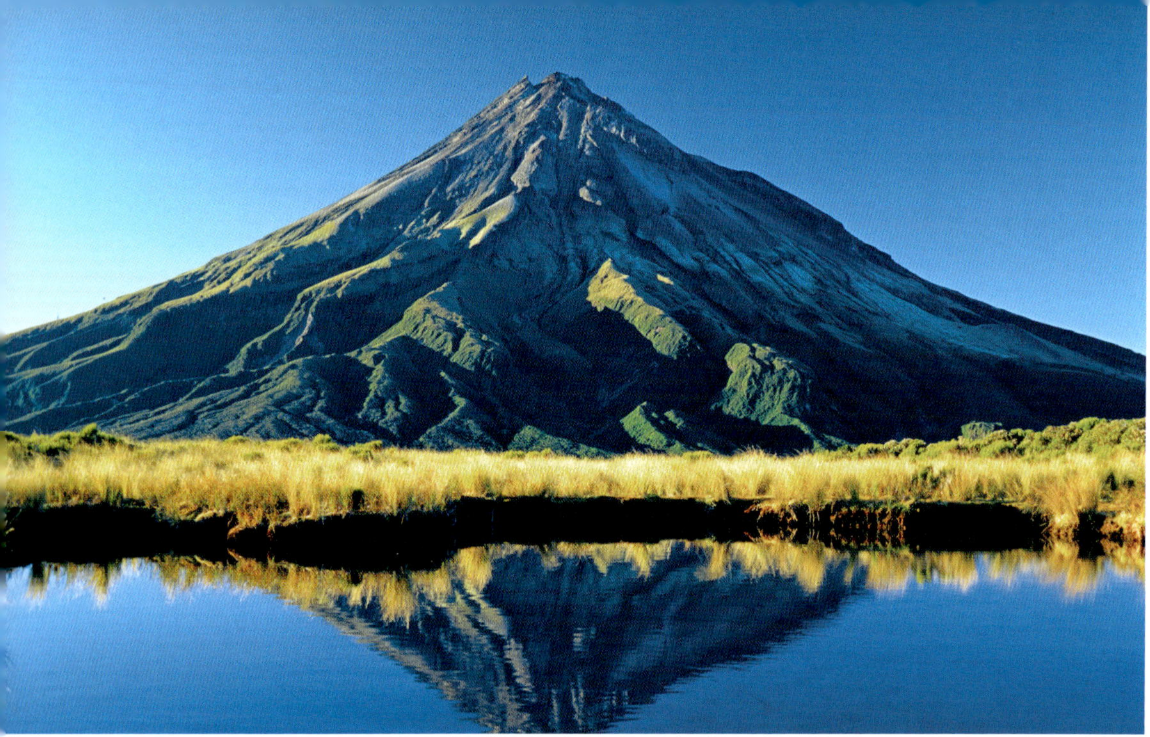

EGMONT

The near-perfect cone of Mt Taranaki, visible for hundreds of kilometres around as it soars high above coastal farmland, is the central focus of Egmont National Park. At the westernmost point of the North Island, this solitary volcano is in the way of the weather, but the high rainfall has its benefits. The rivers run strong and fast, there are many gorgeous waterfalls, and the lakes, wetlands and rainforest have a ready source of sustaining water. The higher slopes of Mt Taranaki are reached by two roads, giving easy access to a network of long and short walking tracks through primeval-looking 'goblin' forest to pools, cascades and – in clear weather – magnificent vistas over the central North Island. Rock climbers and mountaineers like to test themselves on the lava bluffs and in winter on the icy summit.

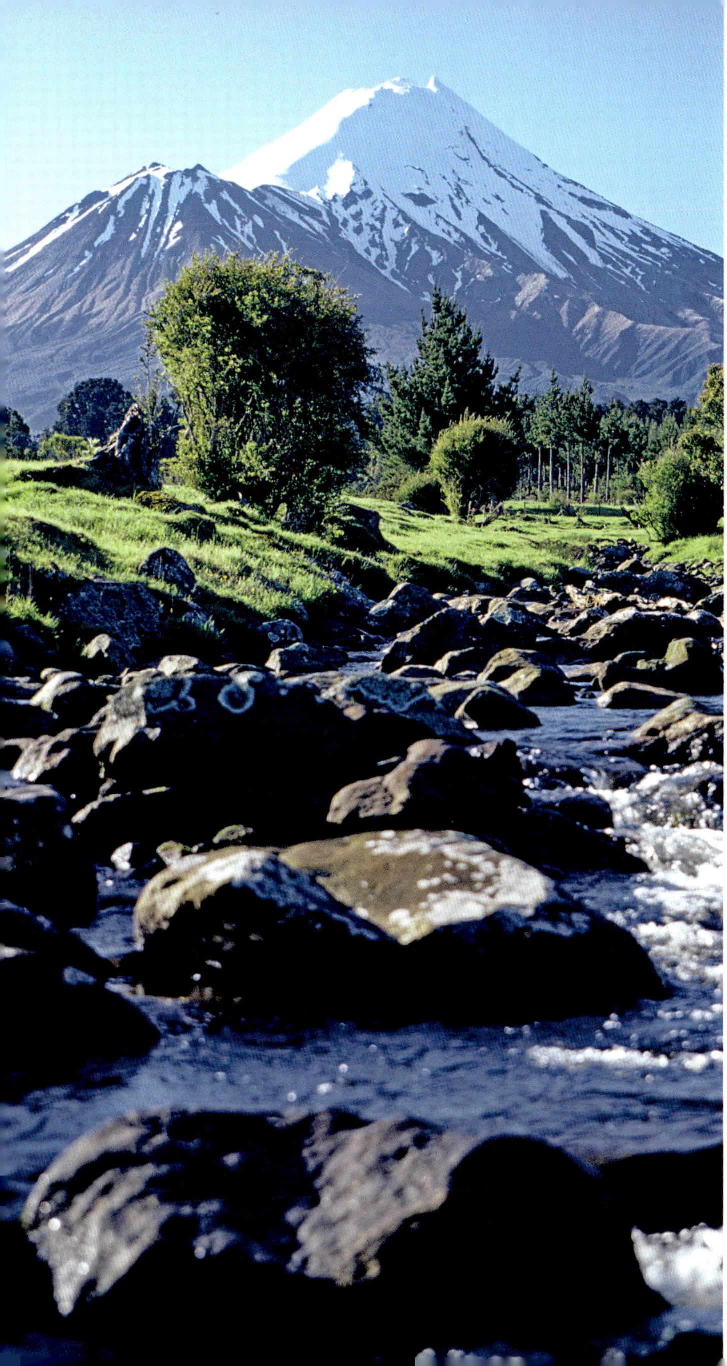

Far left: A tarn high in the Pouakai Range reflects Mt Taranaki's deeply eroded flanks.

Left: The 2518 m peak of Mt Taranaki overshadows the rich farmland around Eltham.

Below: Egmont National Park has its own subspecies of mountain foxglove, which blooms in spring in the herb fields near the bushline.

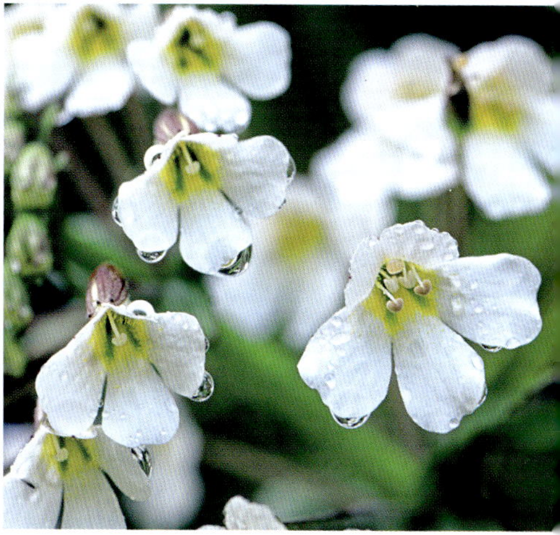

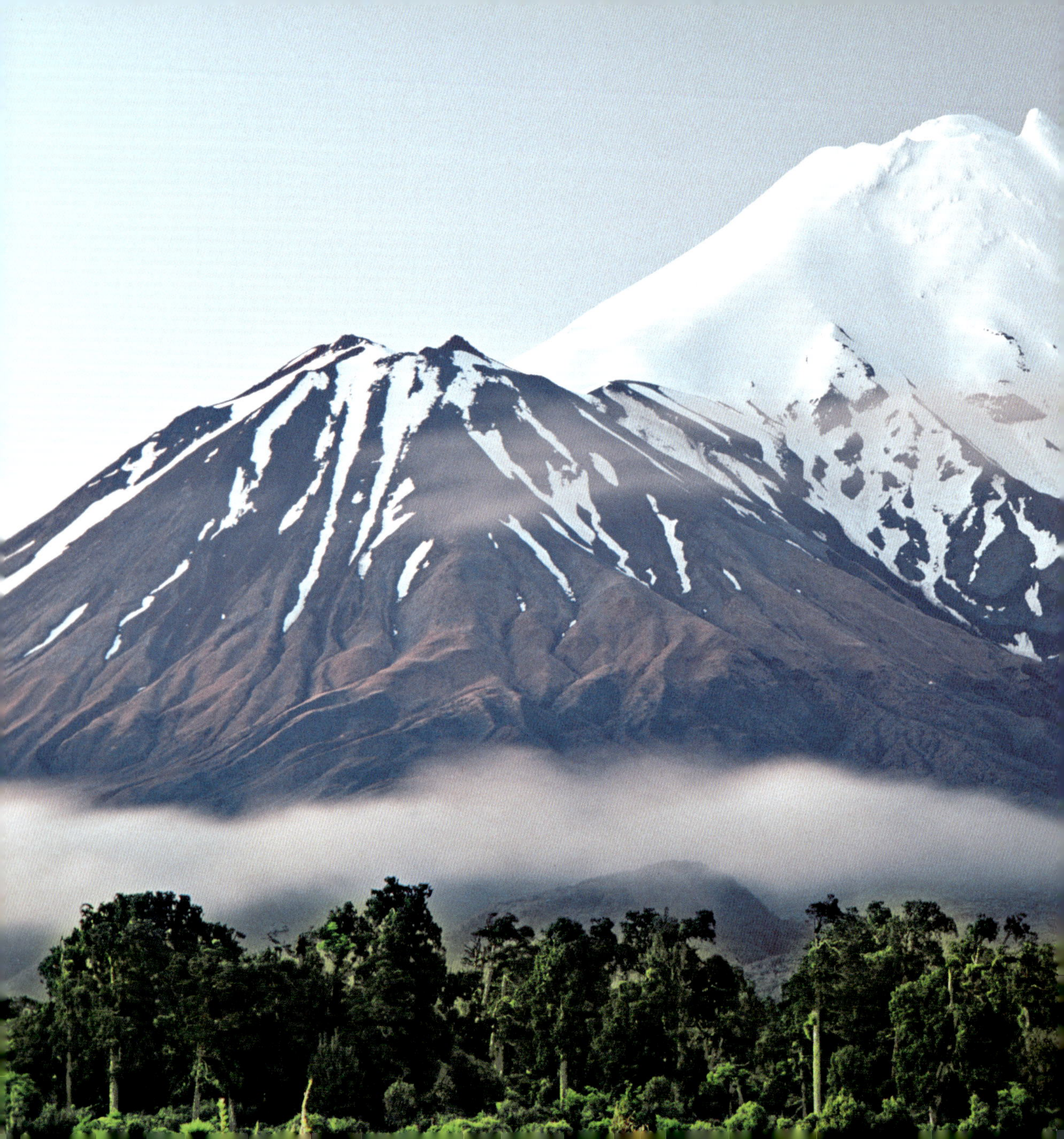

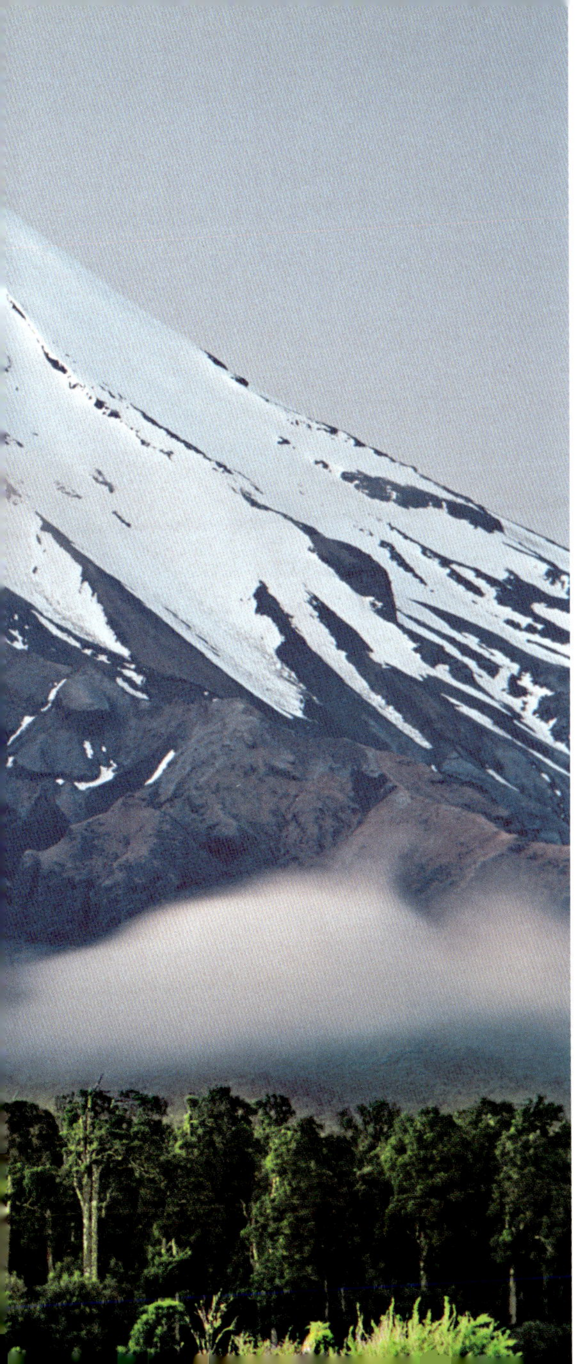

Left: Mt Taranaki takes on a mysterious air after dusk. Fanthams Peak, on the great mountain's south-eastern flank, is a subsidiary volcanic cone that has erupted more recently than the main cone.

Below: In winter Syme Hut on Fanthams Peak, the highest hut in the park, often becomes completely encrusted with ice.

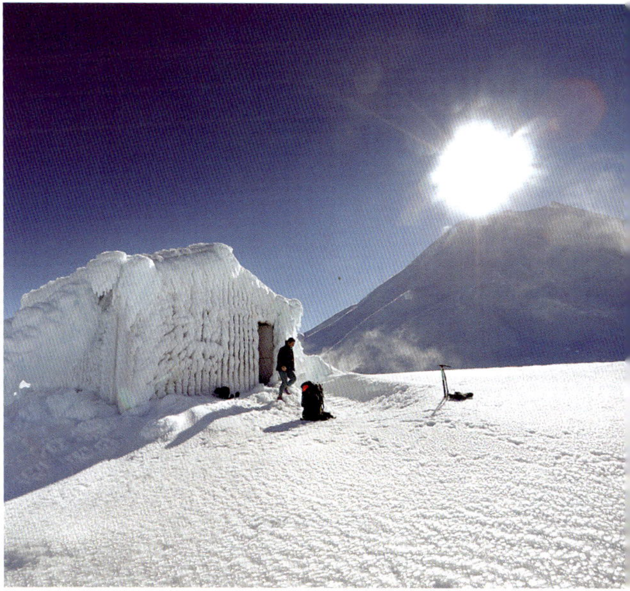

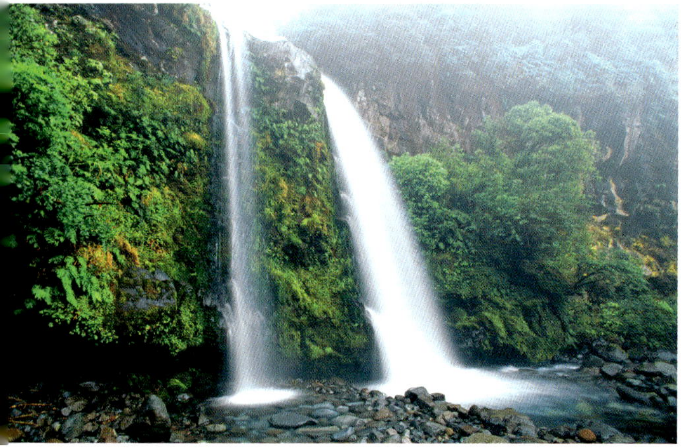

Left: The 18 m Dawson Falls are named for Thomas Dawson, who almost stumbled over them while exploring the Kapuni River.

Below: Mt Taranaki is visible from the coast at Tongaporutu, 70 km away, home to the Three Sisters rock stacks.

Right: Mt Taranaki is a picture of serenity on a calm, clear winter's day. Looks can be deceiving: the weather can change in an instant and the mountain is the most dangerous in New Zealand.

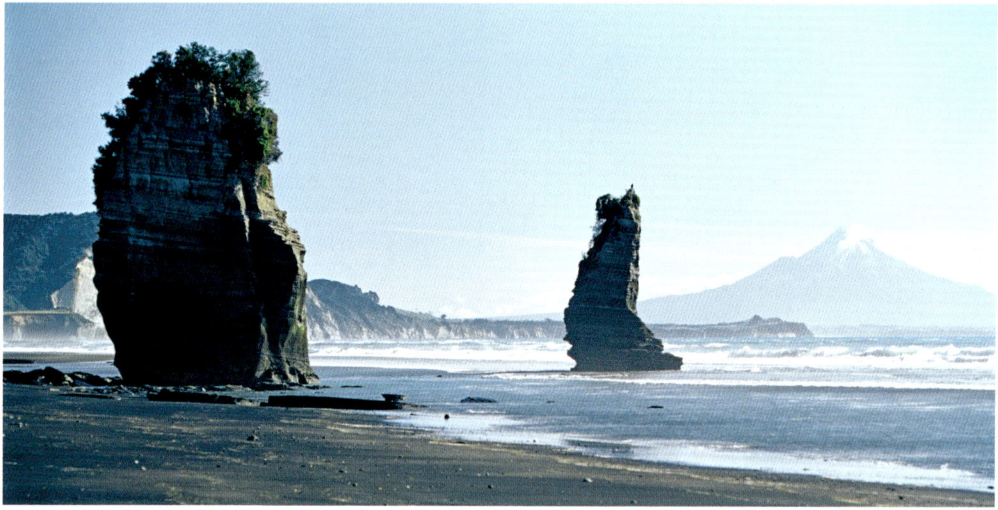

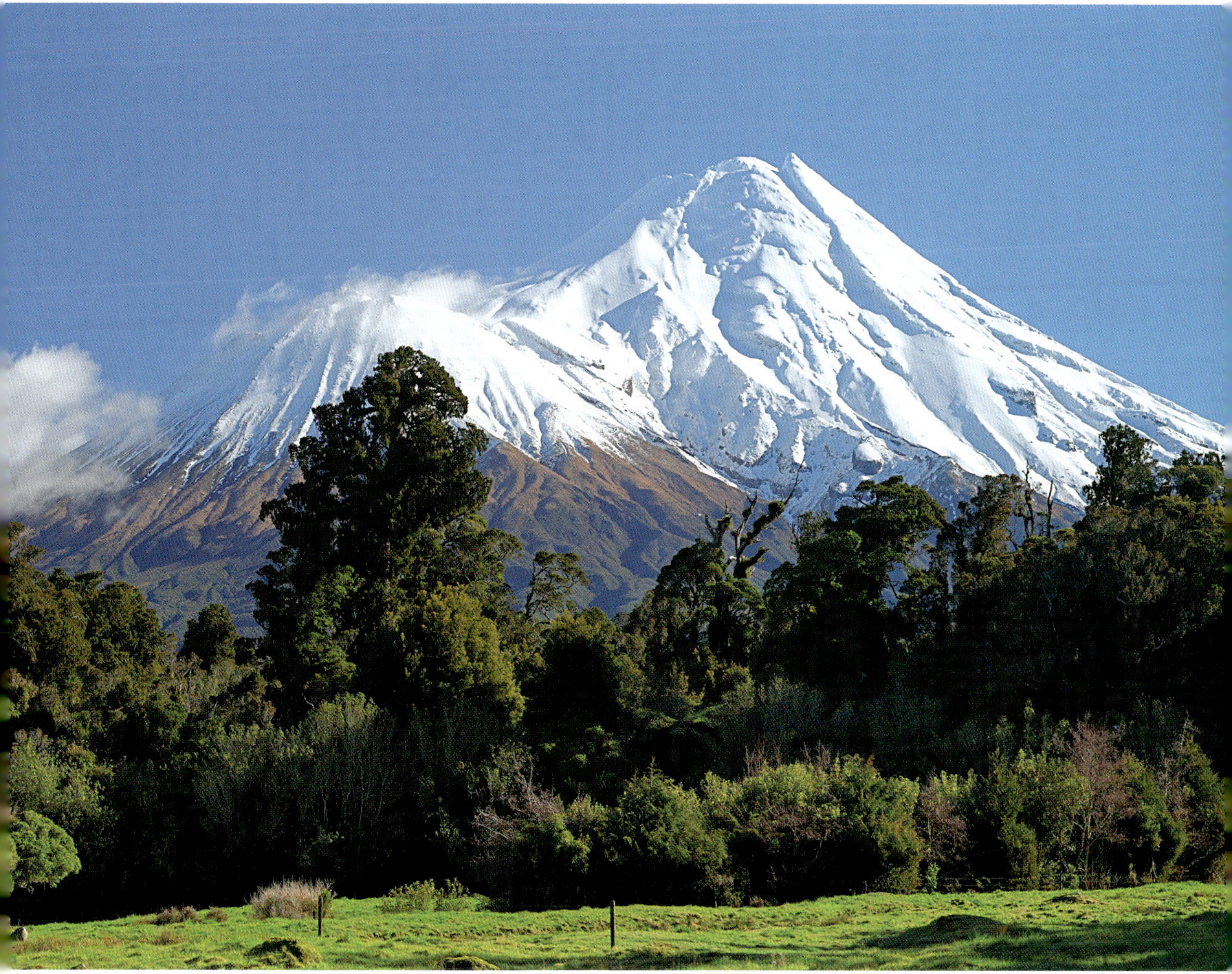

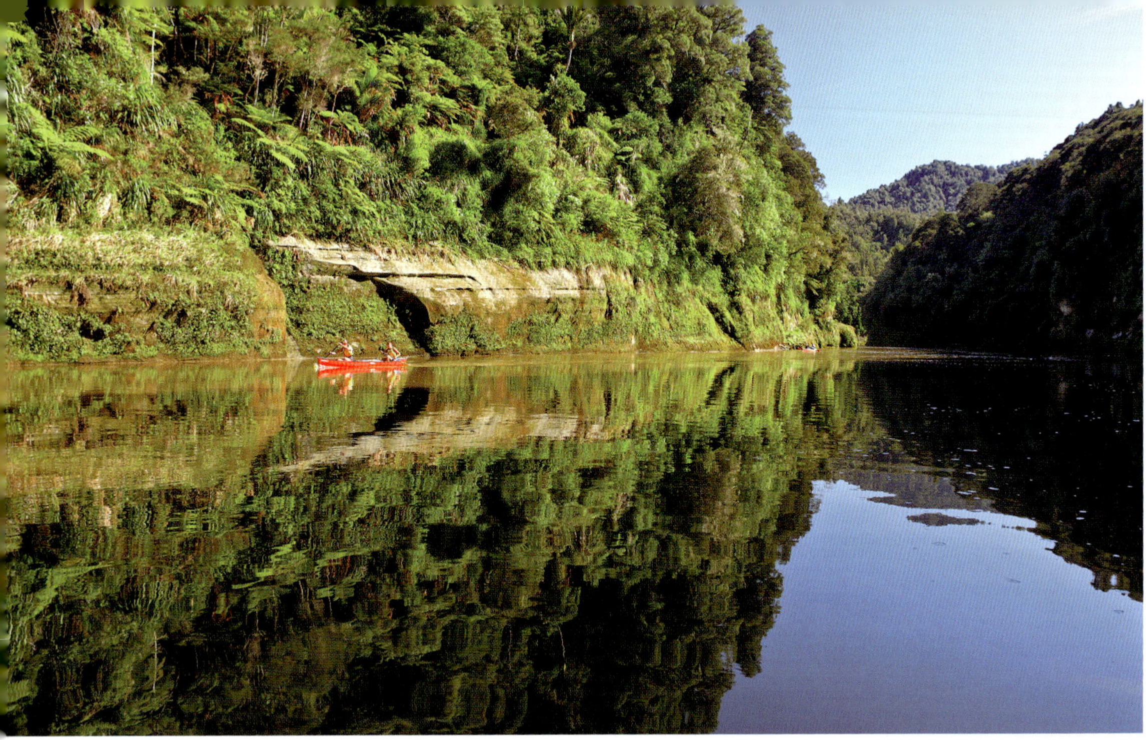

WHANGANUI

The Whanganui River, at the heart of Whanganui National Park, has a human history that is as lively as its rapids-interrupted waters. For centuries it was a key transport route used by Maori in canoes and European settlers in paddle steamers, and pa sites dot its banks in the upper reaches. Today kayakers, canoeists and jetboaters are the main users of the river as it meanders through gorges and under bluffs from the mountains of the central North Island to the Tasman Sea. The river bisects the island's largest remaining tract of native lowland forest, home to North Island brown kiwi and long-tailed bats, and the park is also enjoyed by hikers on multiday walks following old Maori trails and abandoned roads through these wild woodlands.

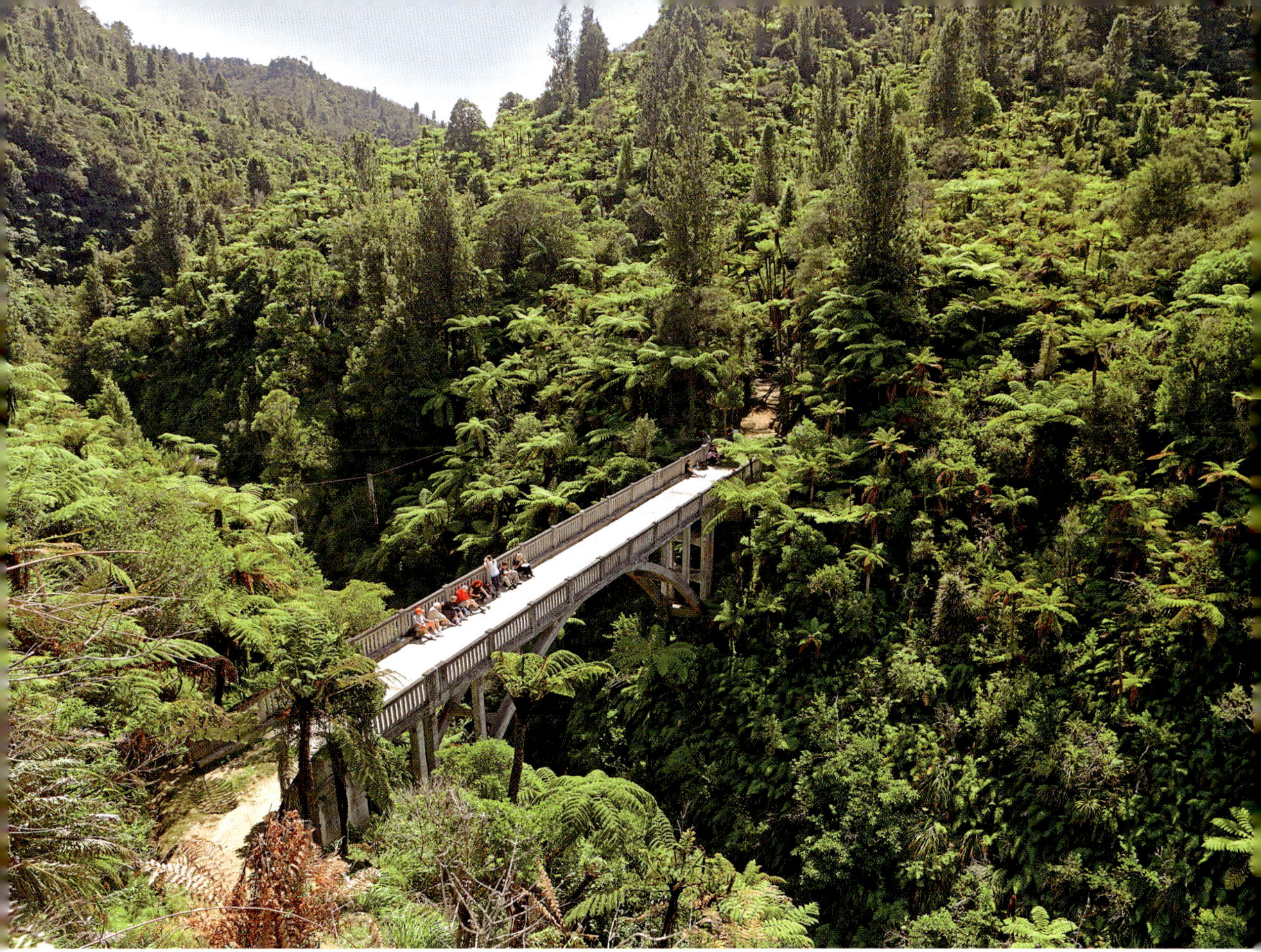

Left: The Whanganui River rises on Mt Tongariro and has worn a channel through the soft stone of the King Country to the sea at Whanganui.

Above: The concrete Bridge to Nowhere has no roads leading to it. It was built in 1936 to link the now-abandoned Mangaparua Valley settlement with the Whanganui River, which was once a main route through the North Island by steamer.

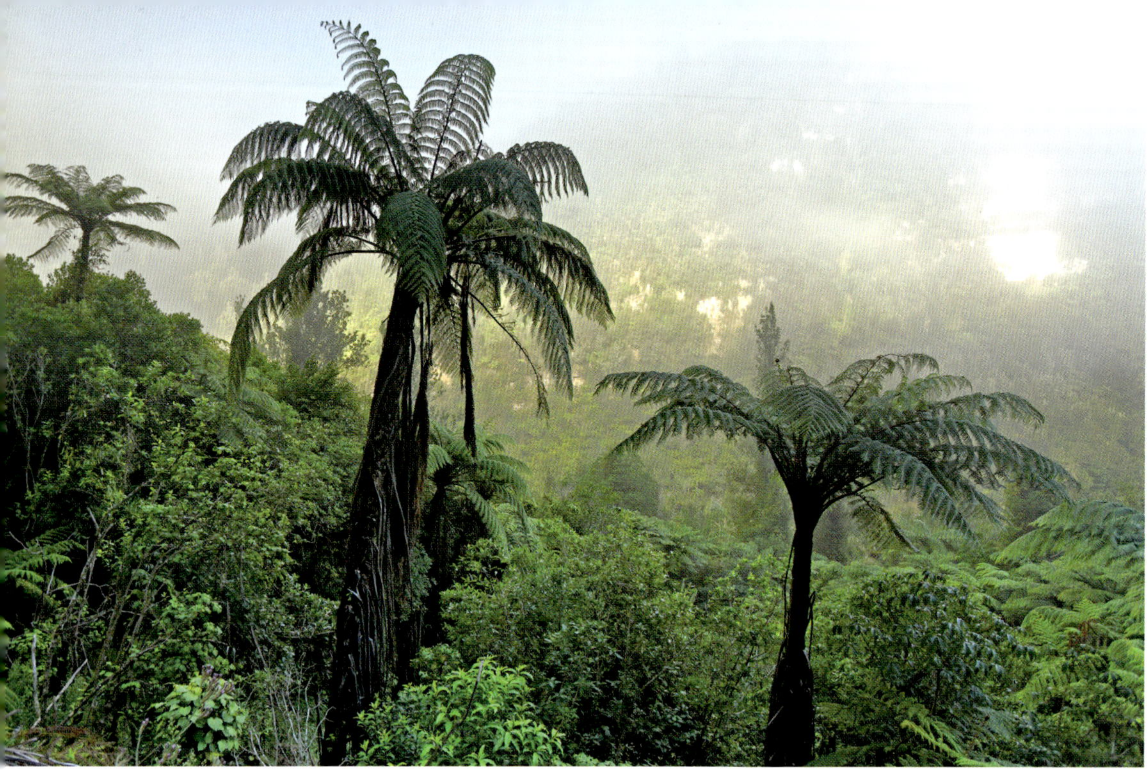

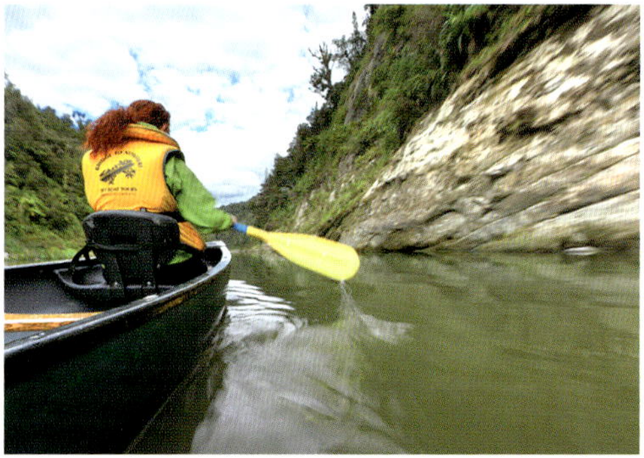

Above: Morning river mist lingers among the mamaku tree ferns.

Left: Canoeists disturb the still waters of the Whanganui River. It takes most paddlers five days to complete the 145 km Whanganui Journey from Taumarunui to Pipiriki.

Right: Ferns and other moisture-loving plants gain a foothold where they can on the steep faces of one of Whanganui National Park's many gorges.

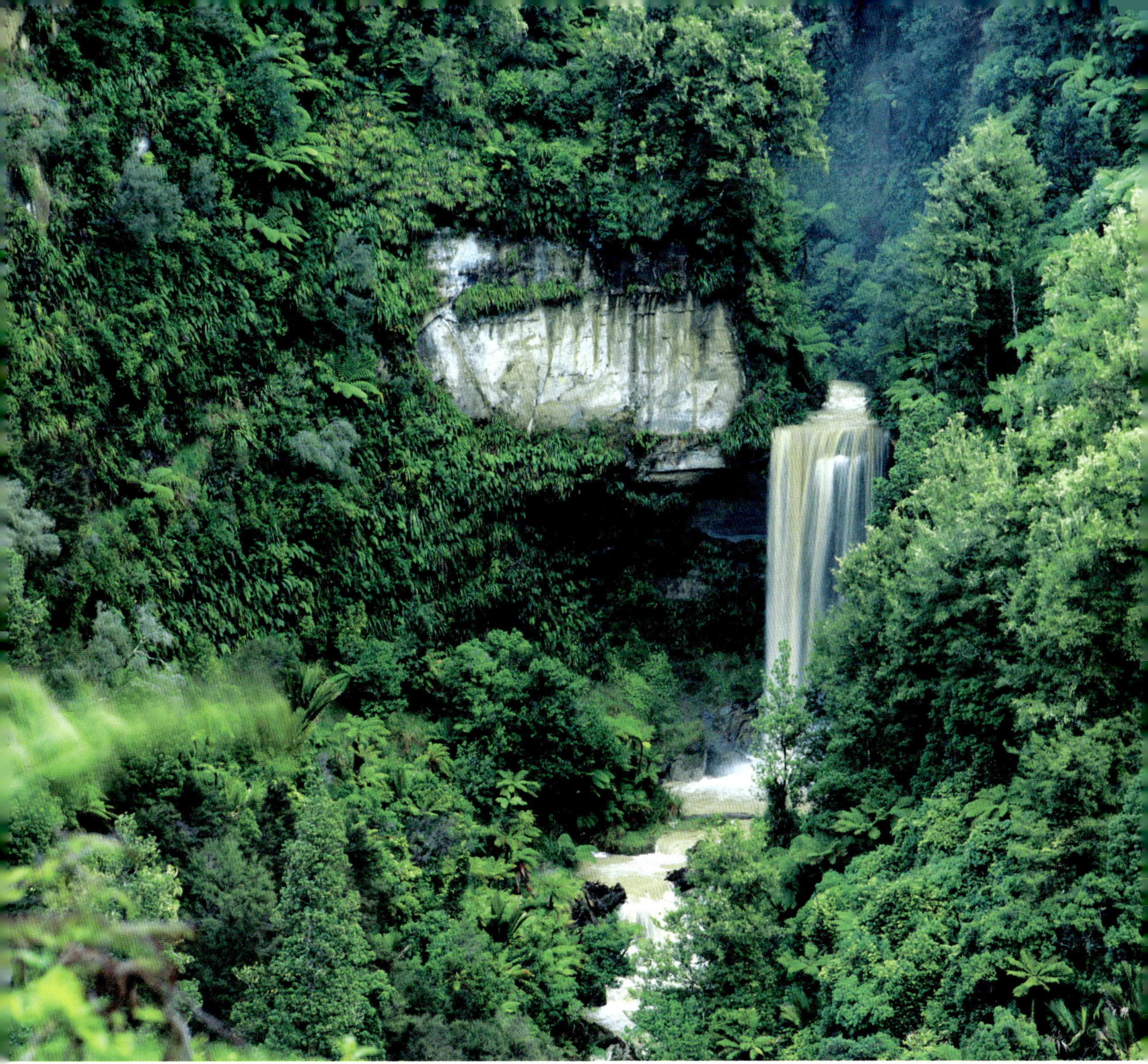

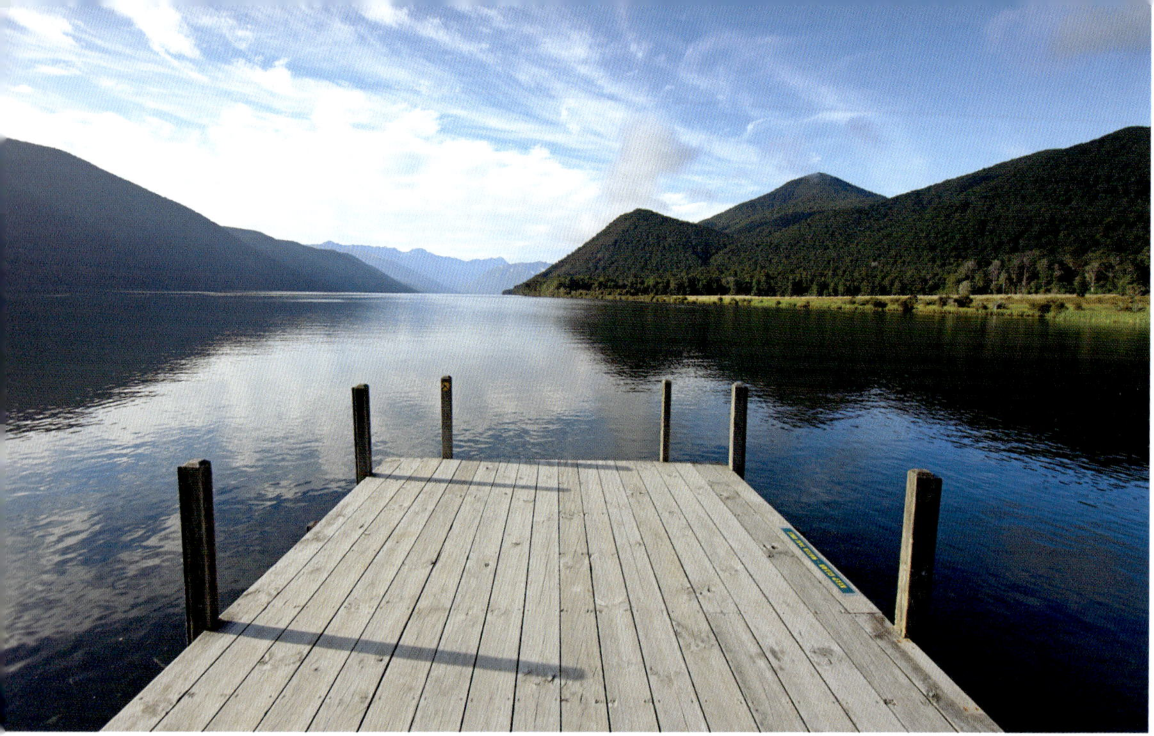

NELSON LAKES

Rotoroa and Rotoiti, the two lakes that gave rise to the name of Nelson Lakes National Park, fill the valleys left by ancient glaciers at the very northern end of the Southern Alps. Easily approached by road, in summer they buzz with the activities of boaties, kayakers and fishers. Beyond the lake shores, however, the quiet descends in peaceful forests, among clear lakes, streams and waterfalls, on steep mountainsides and, above the distinct bushline, in alpine fell fields. The honeydew beech forest teems with bird life. This is especially true within the Rotoiti Nature Recovery Project, where kaka, bellbirds and great spotted kiwi are kept safe from predators.

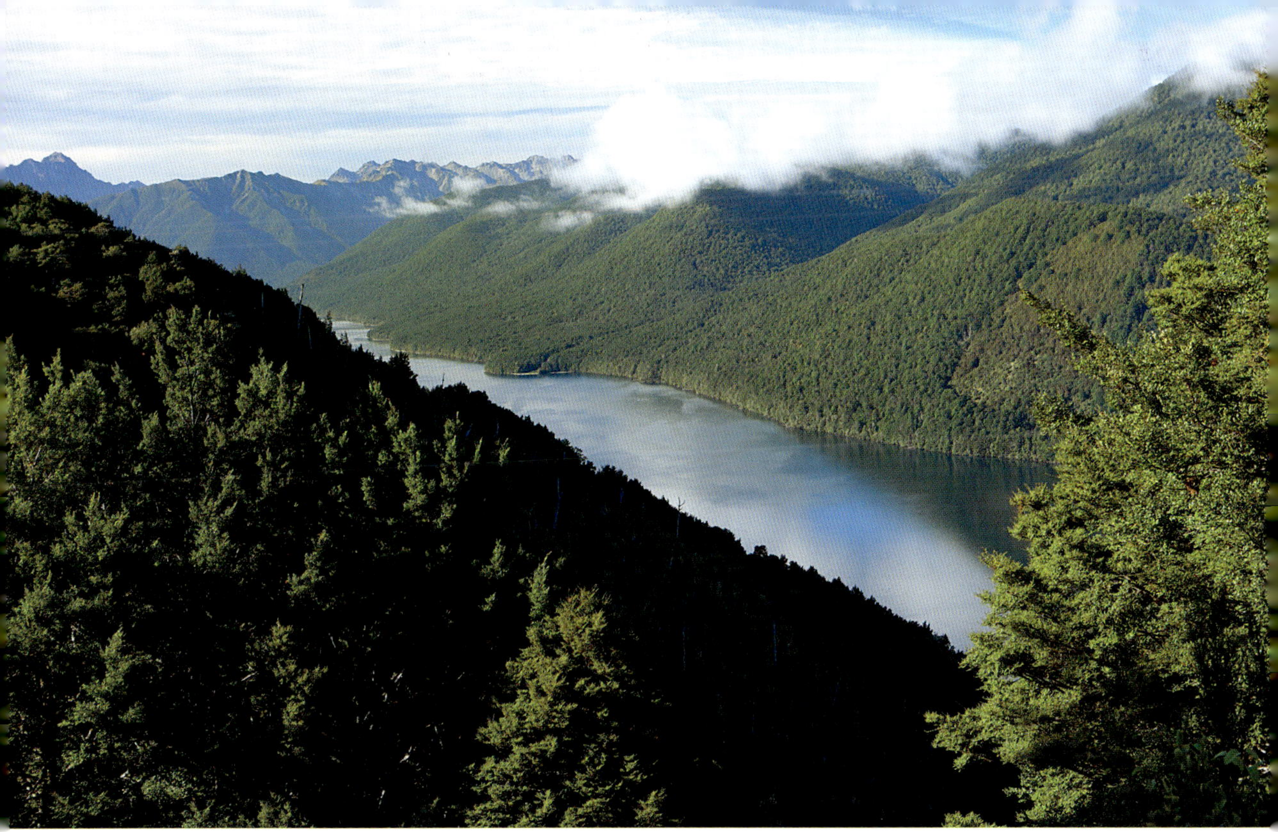

Left: Rotoroa is the larger of the two great lakes of Nelson Lakes National Park. The lake and the rivers feeding it offer excellent trout fishing.

Above: Rotoroa is set among honeydew beech forest below the Travers Range.

Right: Rotoiti – the name means 'small lake' – is sheltered by mountains to the west and east.

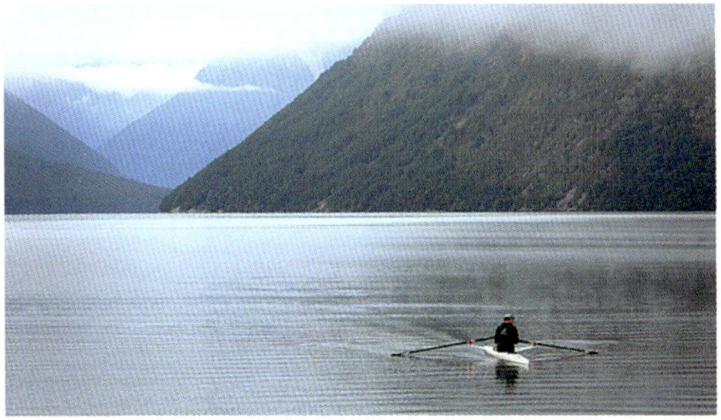

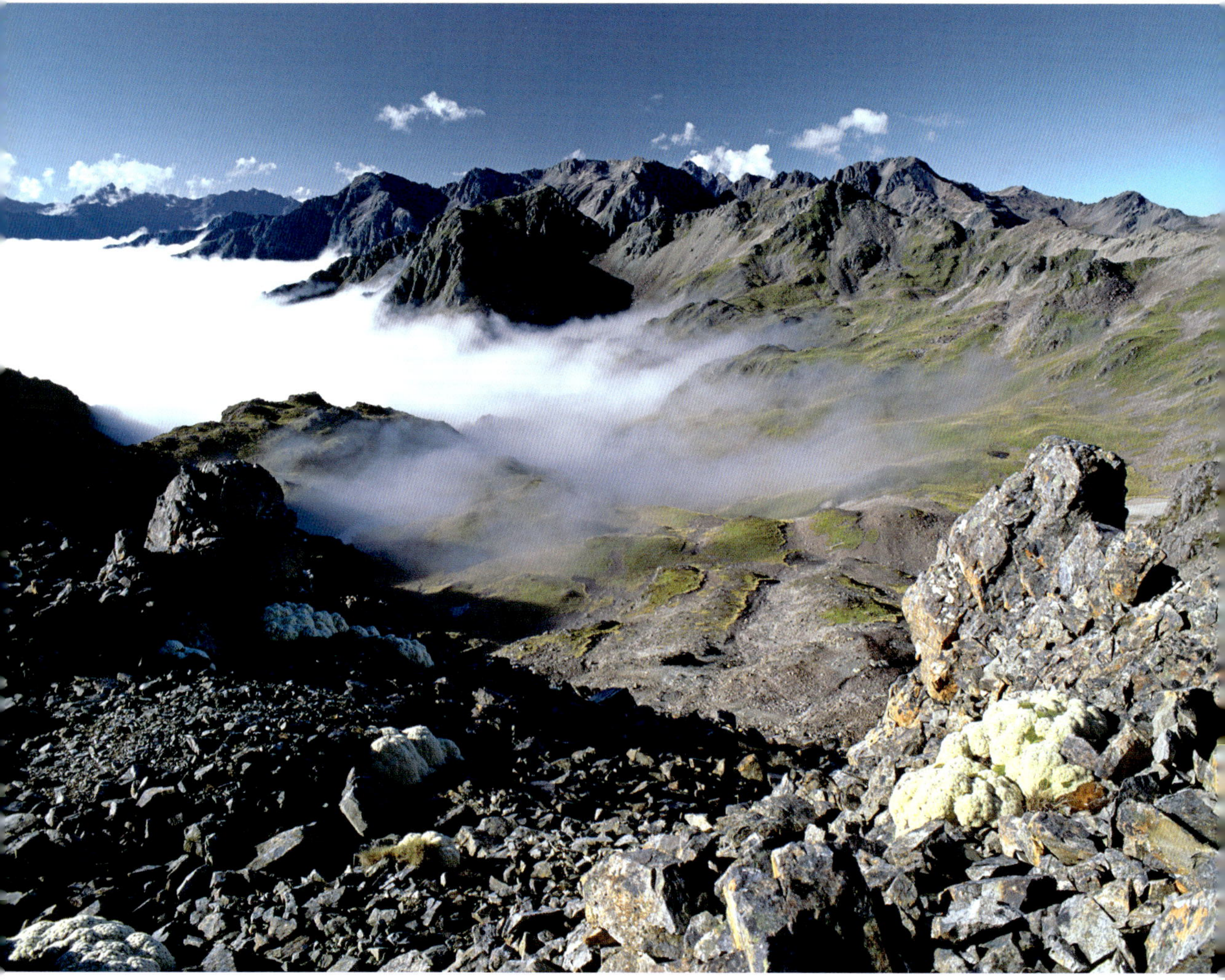

Left: The bleak ramparts of the Travers Range near Lake Angelus seem to offer little to sustain life, but the remarkable vegetable sheep (foreground), a dense, cushion-like alpine plant, somehow finds nutrition in the scree.

Right: Scarlet mistletoe/korukoru is especially vulnerable to possums; its presence indicates that the forest is in good shape, and its nectar is an important breeding food for many of our forest birds.

Below: This lonely spot on the Robert Ridge offers a vista over the mist of Travers Valley and Lake Rotoiti.

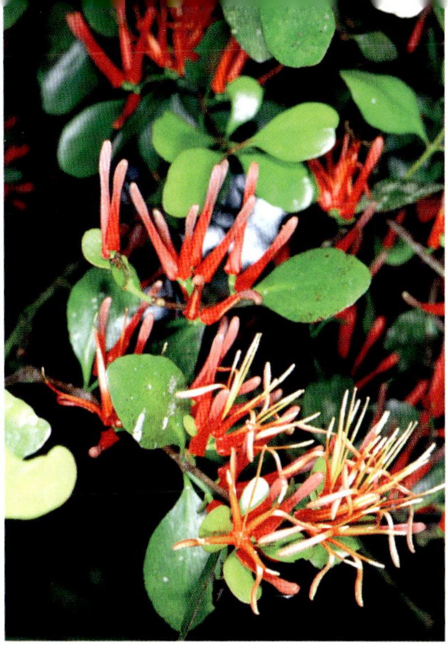

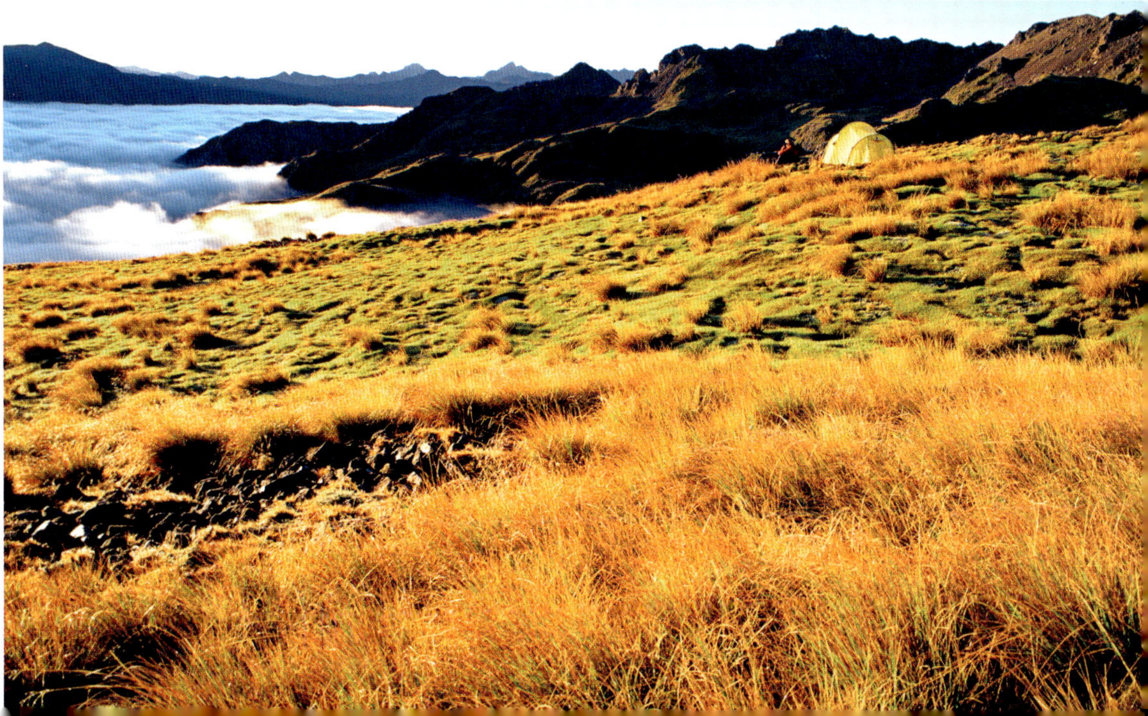

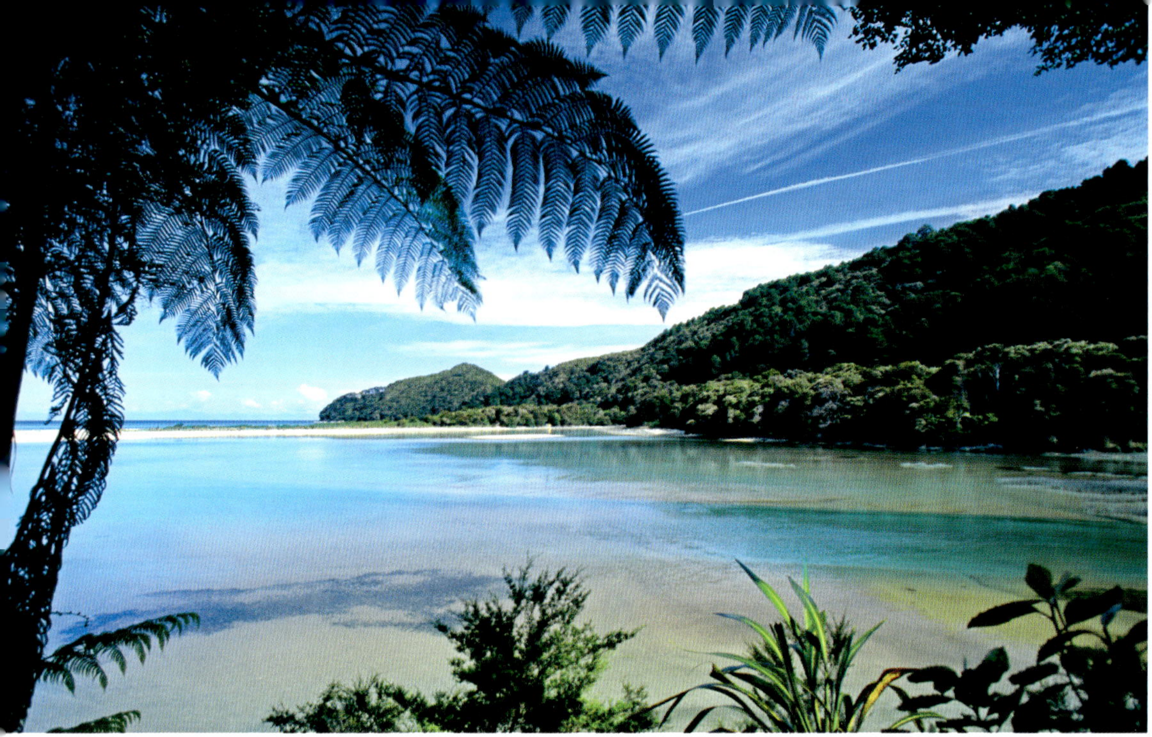

ABEL TASMAN

The smallest of New Zealand's national parks, Abel Tasman is also one of the best loved. It is enjoyed by locals and visitors for its perfect crescent beaches of golden sand, granite cliffs, lagoons, wetlands and estuaries. Wildlife along the coast includes penguins, seals, dolphins and seabirds. A Great Walk provides a gentle pedestrian tour through the park's sea edge, while kayakers explore bays that can only be reached by sea. Among the regenerating beech forest of the less-frequented inland part, fascinating rocky outcrops of limestone and marble are scattered about and immense cave systems thread their way through the ground beneath your feet. The park is named after the first European to find New Zealand, a Dutch explorer who made contact with Maori in Golden Bay in 1642.

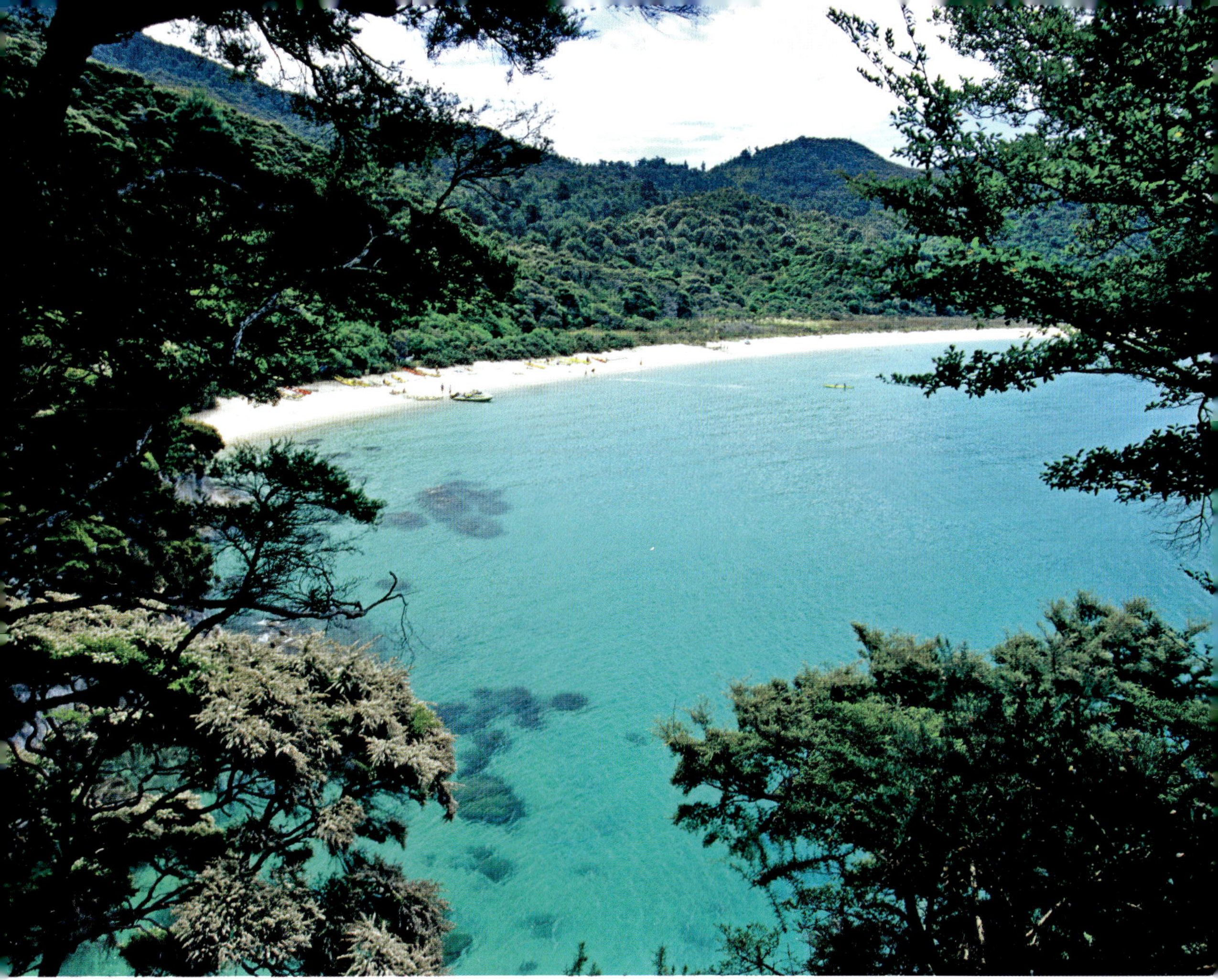

Left: The Abel Tasman Coast Track visits many peaceful bays and sandy beaches. Bark Bay is a popular overnight stop for both walkers and kayakers.

Above: Surrounded by regenerating forest, the remote beach at Onetahuti is a gorgeous sweep of golden sand, making a soft landing for water craft.

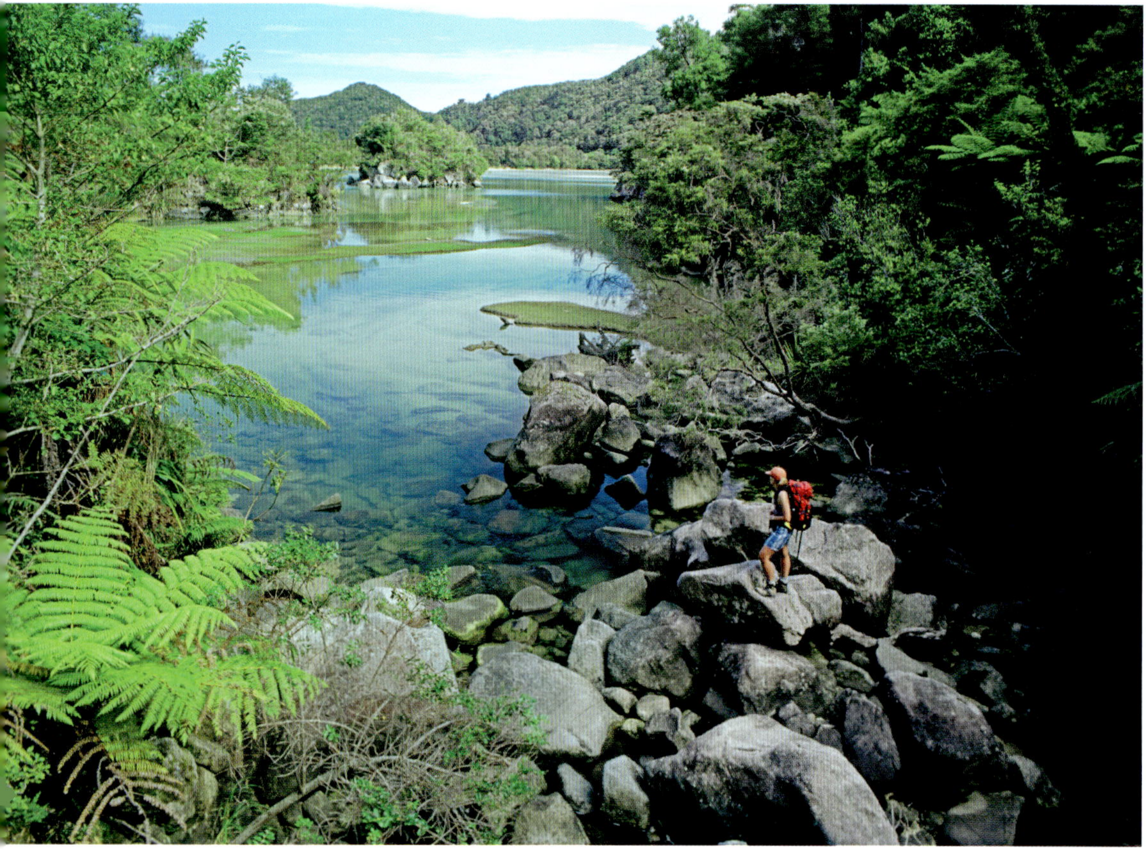

Above: Mosquito Bay is the perfect spot to cool off on a hot summer's day. The only way to reach this tiny inlet north of Bark Bay is by sea.

Right: The sun rises behind Reef Point, off Onetahuti. All wildlife here – fish, shellfish, dolphins, seals and birds – is protected within the Tonga Island Marine Reserve.

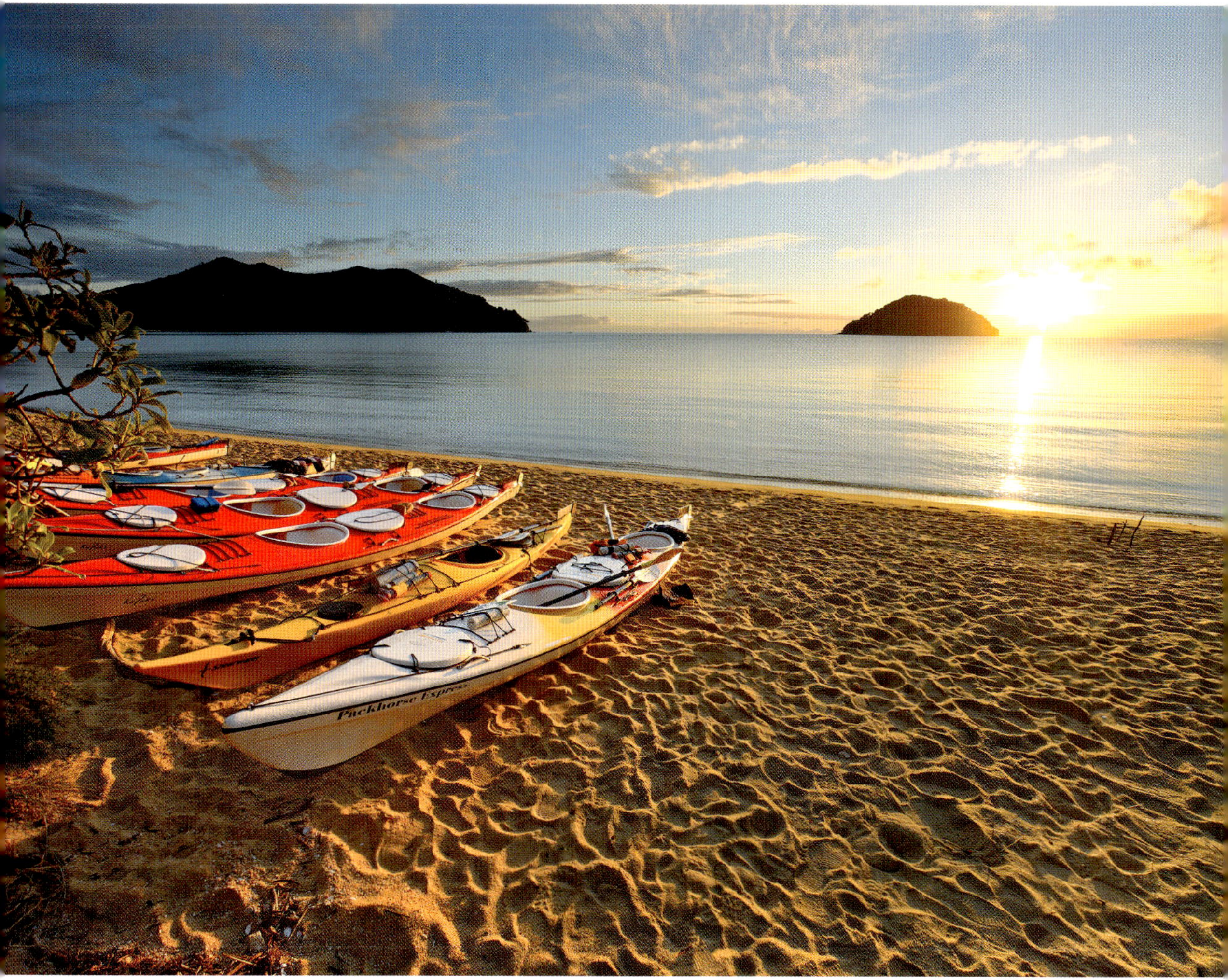
Packhorse Express

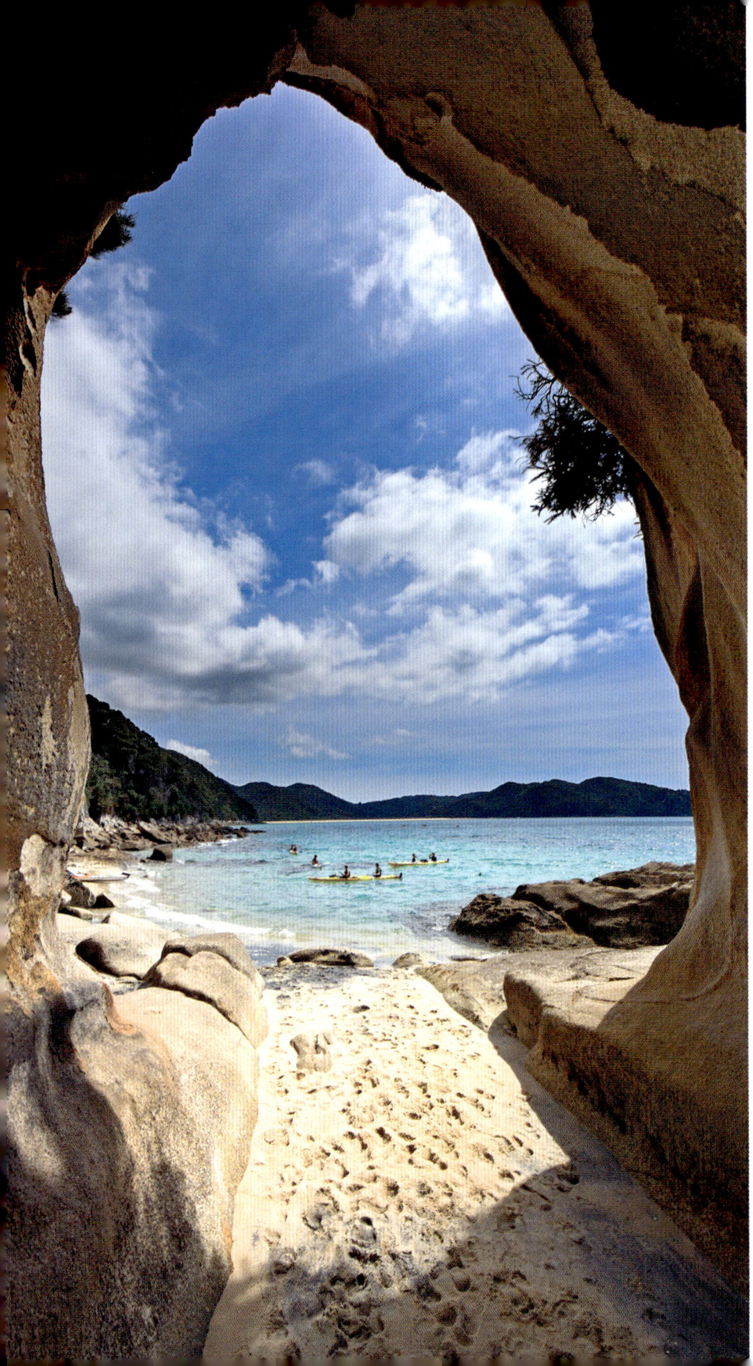

Left: At Arch Point the sea has worn the granite rock into strange forms, including a tunnel through the cliff.

Below: The Abel Tasman Coast Track, one of the best maintained of the Great Walks, crosses Huffam Stream at Bark Bay.

Right: Bark Bay is sheltered from the weather by bush-clad hills.

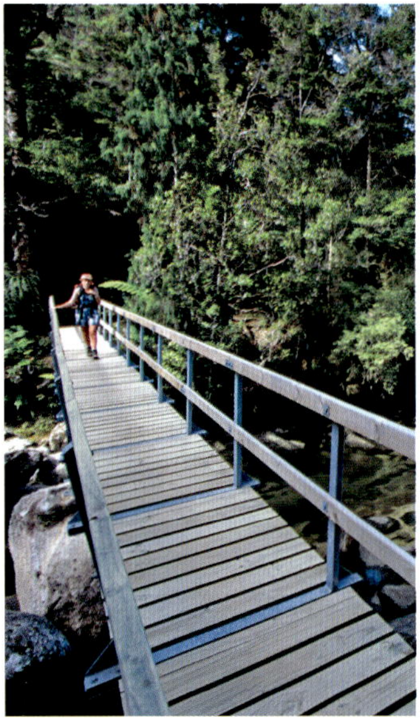

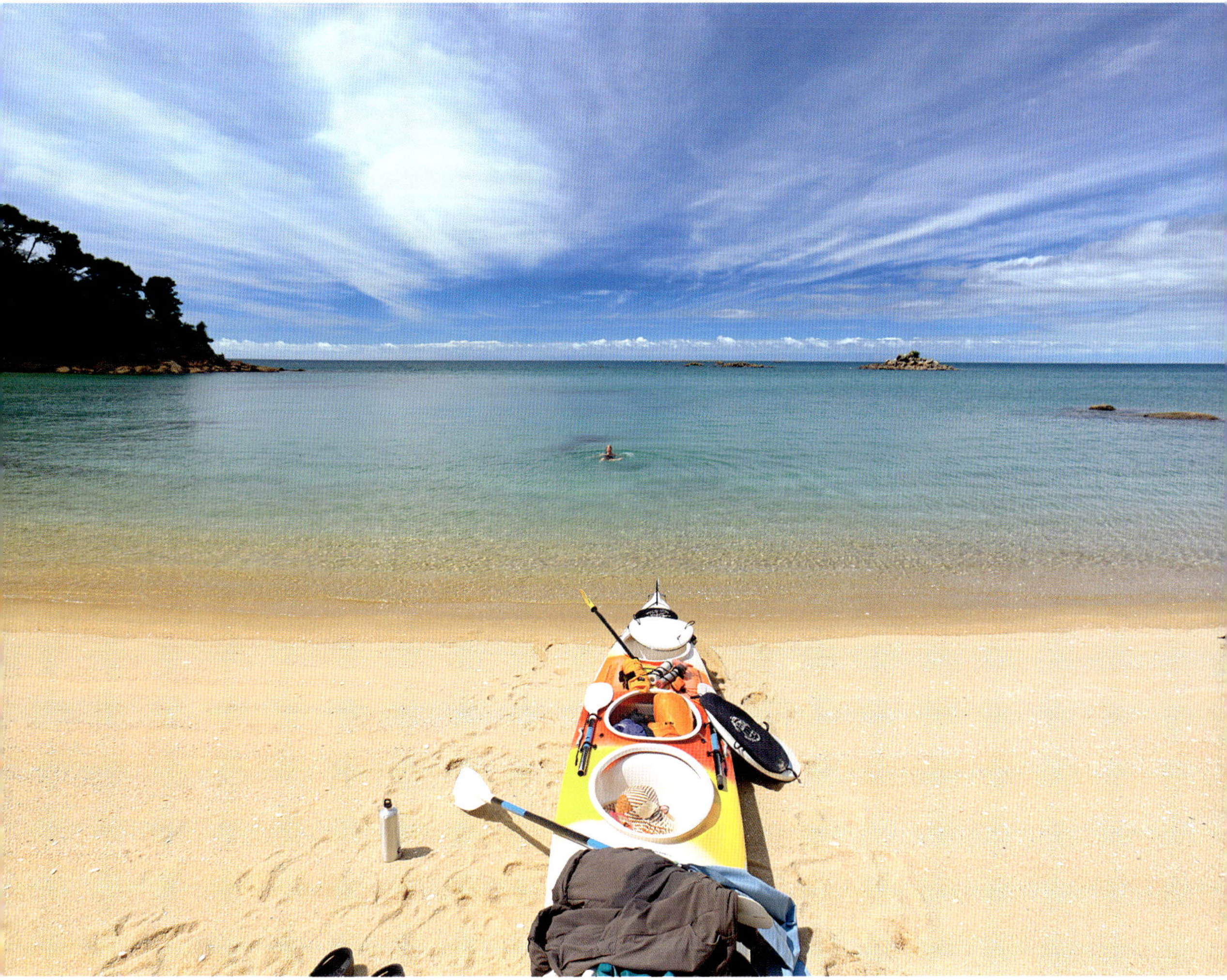

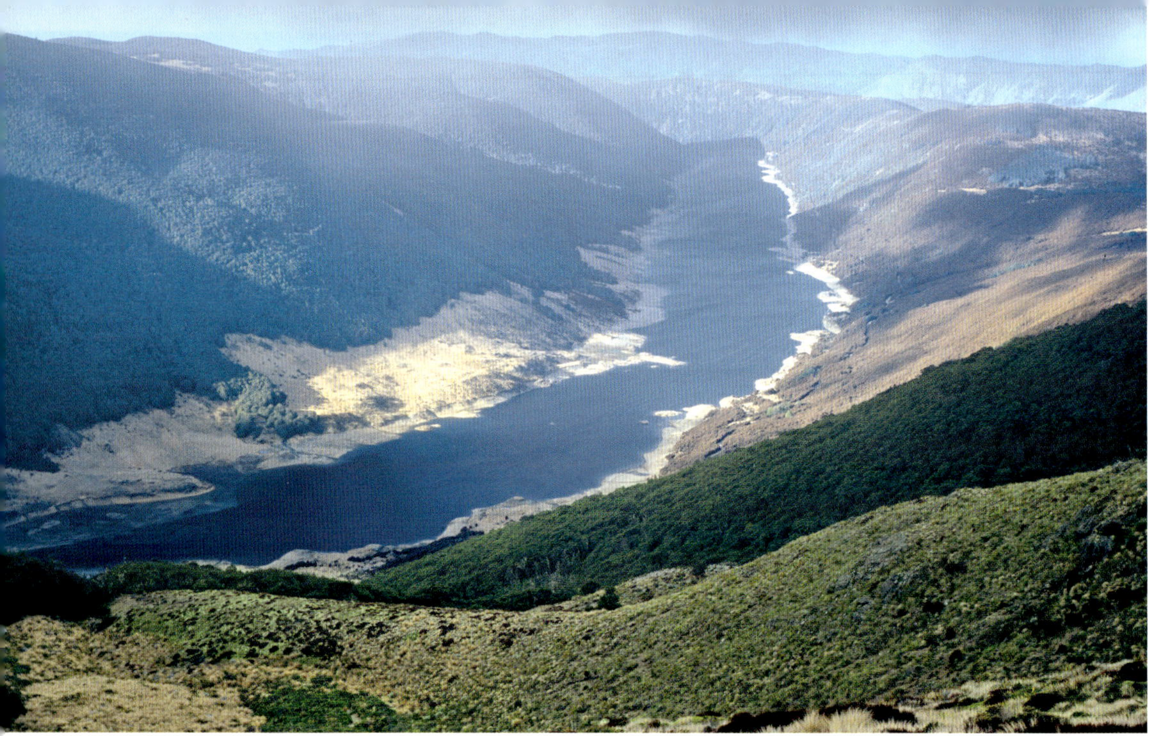

KAHURANGI

The name Kahurangi has a number of meanings, including 'treasured possession'. It is a resonant description for this huge and diverse park, which has the richest native flora of all of New Zealand's national parks as well as some of the most exceptional landforms. This provides a varied habitat for a wide range of wild creatures, among them great spotted kiwi, giant weta and kaka. Beech forest dominates in the mountainous east but lush rainforest takes over to the west and nikau palms give a Pacific Island feel. The landscape takes in alpine tops, marble mountains, glacier-scoured valleys and lakes, high tablelands, limestone caves and a rugged coastline. Some is untracked wilderness but some is crisscrossed by tracks, making life easy for walkers.

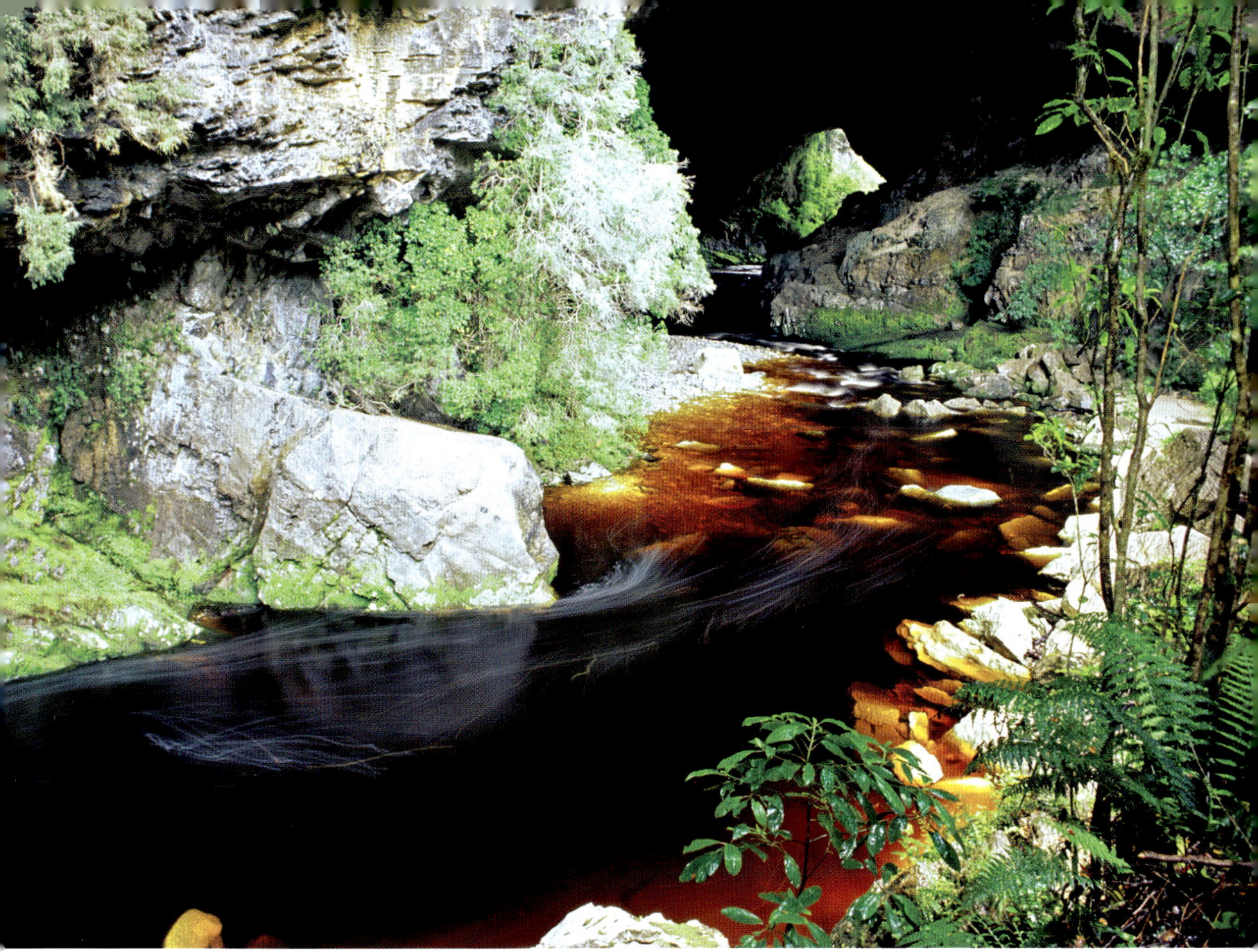

Left: The Cobb Reservoir occupies a classic glacial valley carved during the ice ages. The dam access road is the starting point for a number of walks: to mining relics, historic huts and lakes, and up to the mountain tops.

Above: The Oparara River, seen here entering the huge Oparara Arch, is stained brown by tannin from organic matter. The 35-million-year-old limestone of the Oparara Basin has been sculpted by water into an amazing network of caves and channels.

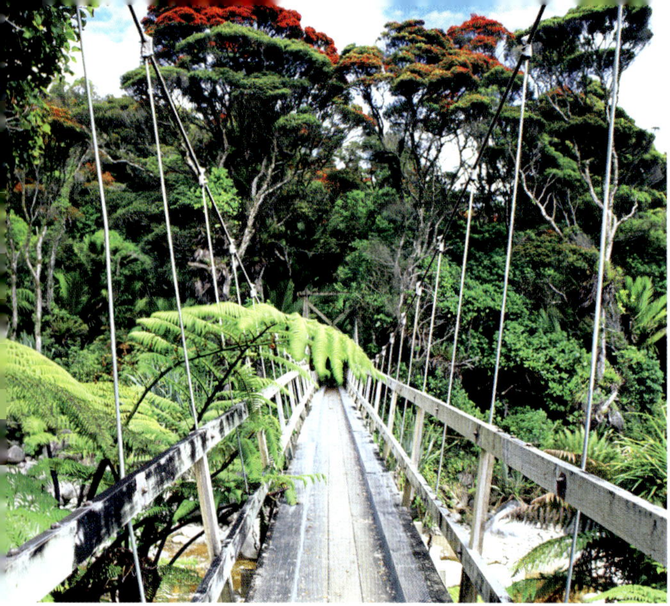

Left: Swing bridges that wobble as you walk are a feature of tramping in New Zealand. The bridge over Wekakura Creek on the coastal section of the Heaphy Track is just one example.

Below: At Koura Beach the full force of the Tasman Sea has deposited a bank of boulders. The Heaphy Track runs along this windswept coastline for 14 km.

Right: Scotts Beach stretches north from Kohaihai Bluff, at the western end of the Heaphy Track.

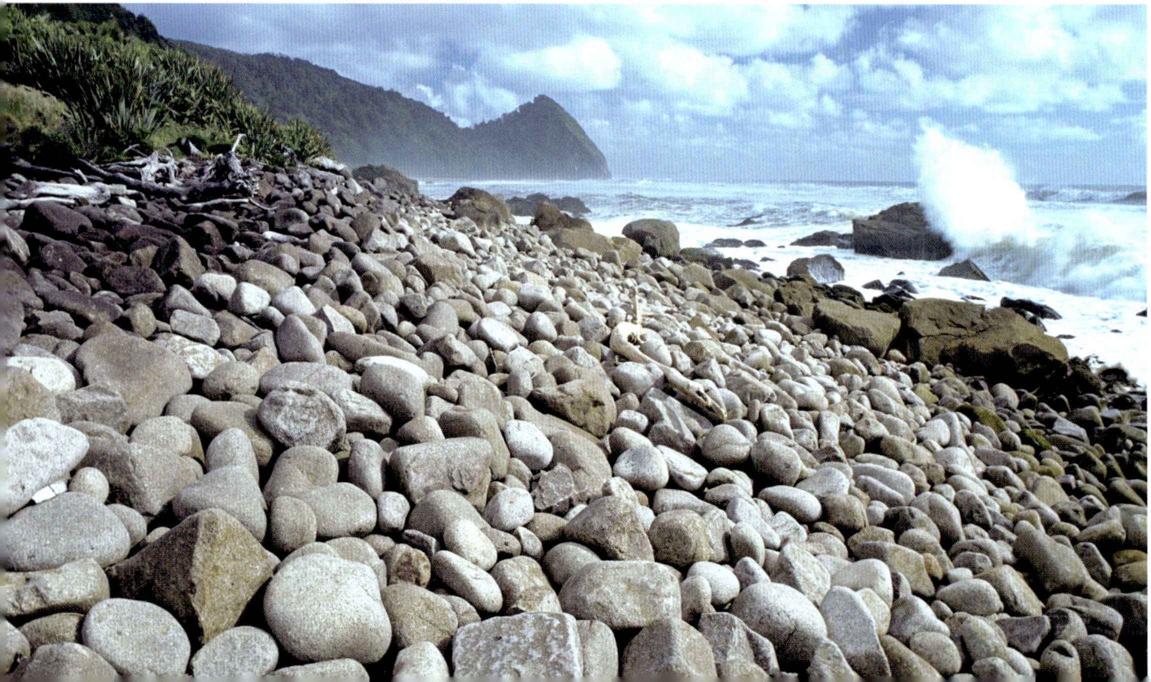

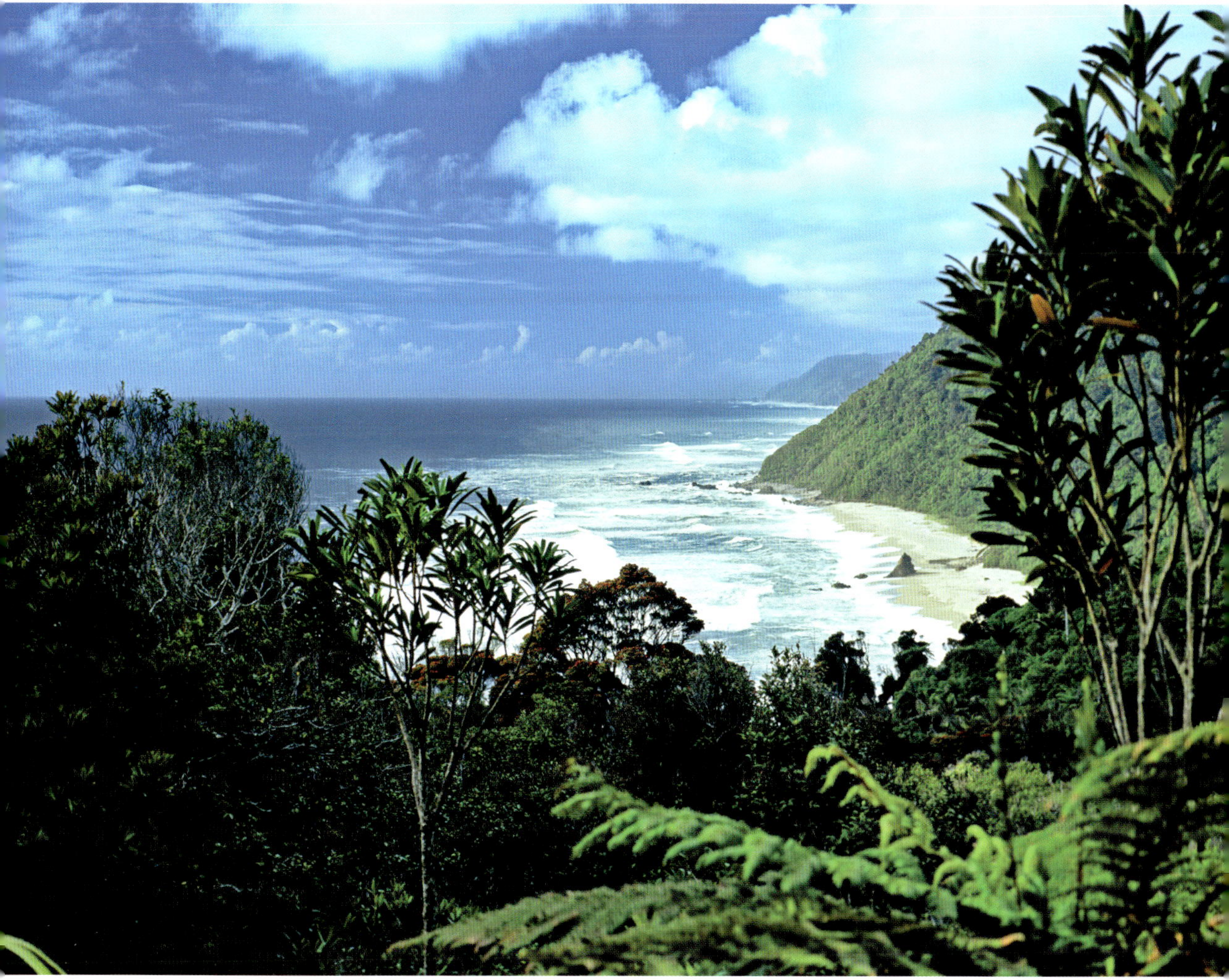

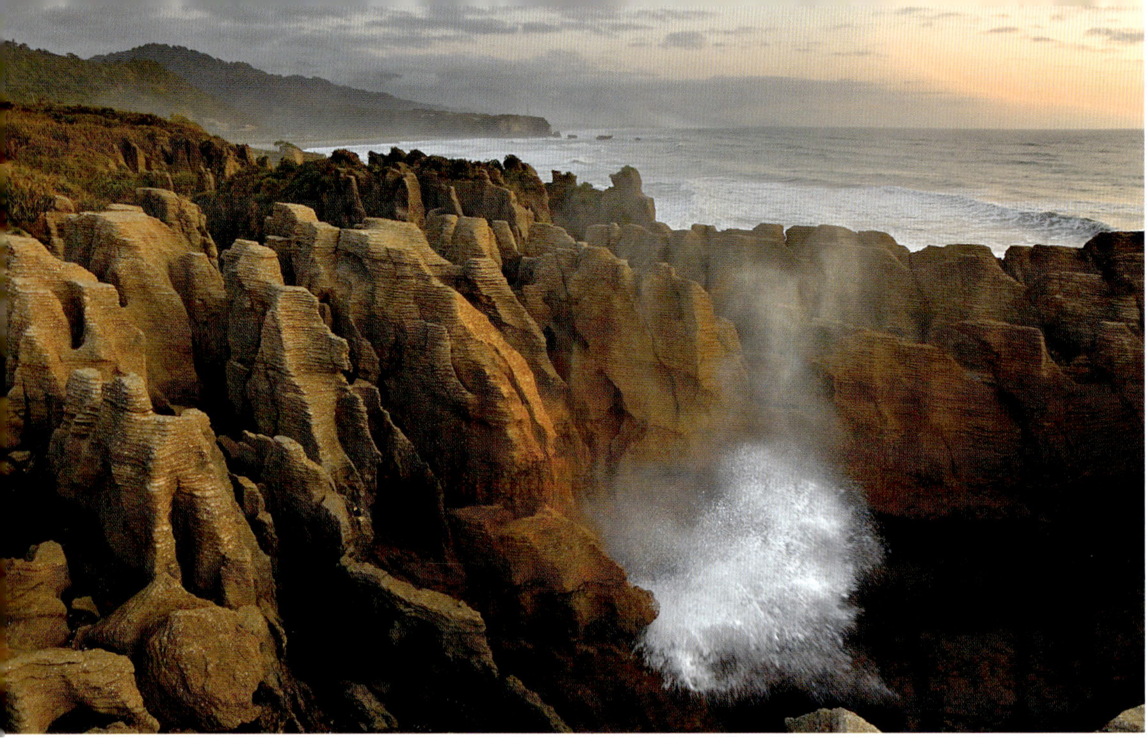

PAPAROA

Paparoa National Park was created in 1987 after a campaign to protect a chunk of West Coast land from mining and logging. It may be one of the smallest of the national parks but, thanks to some remarkable pancake rocks and blowholes, it is one of the most visited. The park has the region's classic features of a dramatic wild coast and dense green forests of beech, rata, ferns and nikau. The Paparoa Range drops more than 1000 m in altitude in just 10 km, and carved into its slopes are amazing limestone canyons and caves. The bird life is diverse: great spotted kiwi make their home here and the only breeding colony of Westland petrels can be found south of Punakaiki.

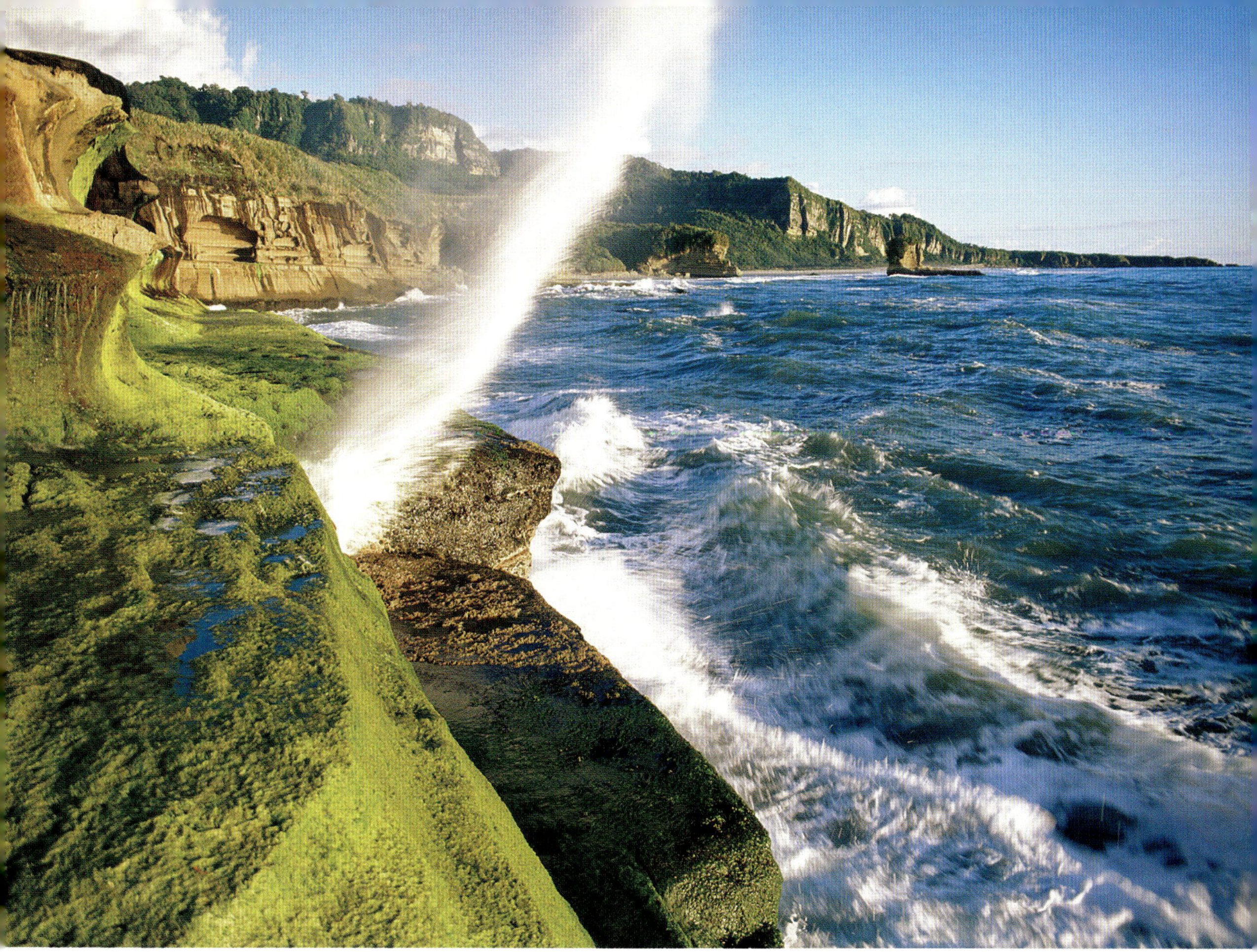

Left: At the Pancake Rocks of Dolomite Point, near Punakaiki, the sea surges through layered limestone stacks, arches and sea chambers that have been eroded into curious shapes by the action of rain, wind and seawater.

Above: The blowholes at Punakaiki put on a spectacular show as the sea thunders into the passages and fissures and escapes in a burst of spray and foam.

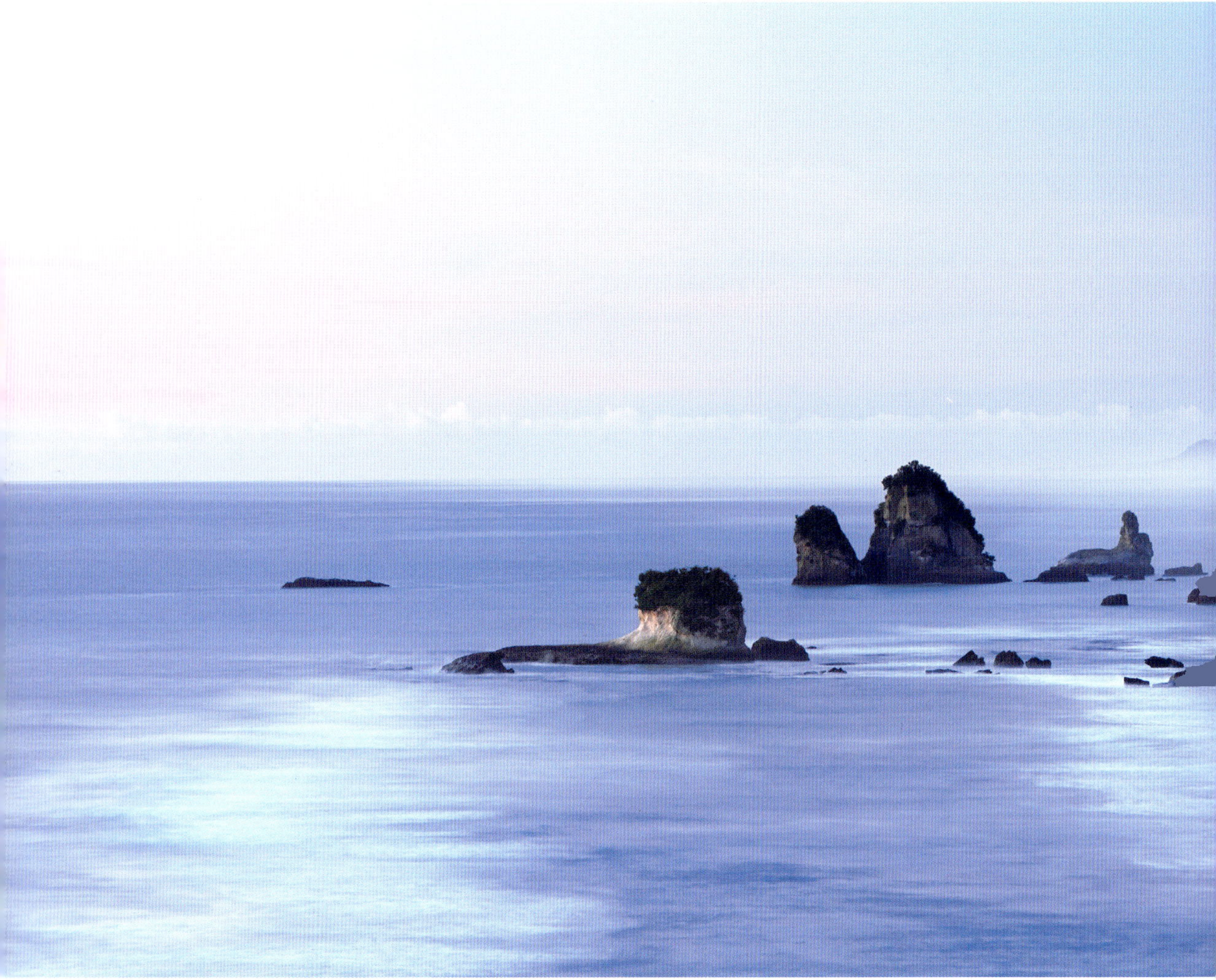

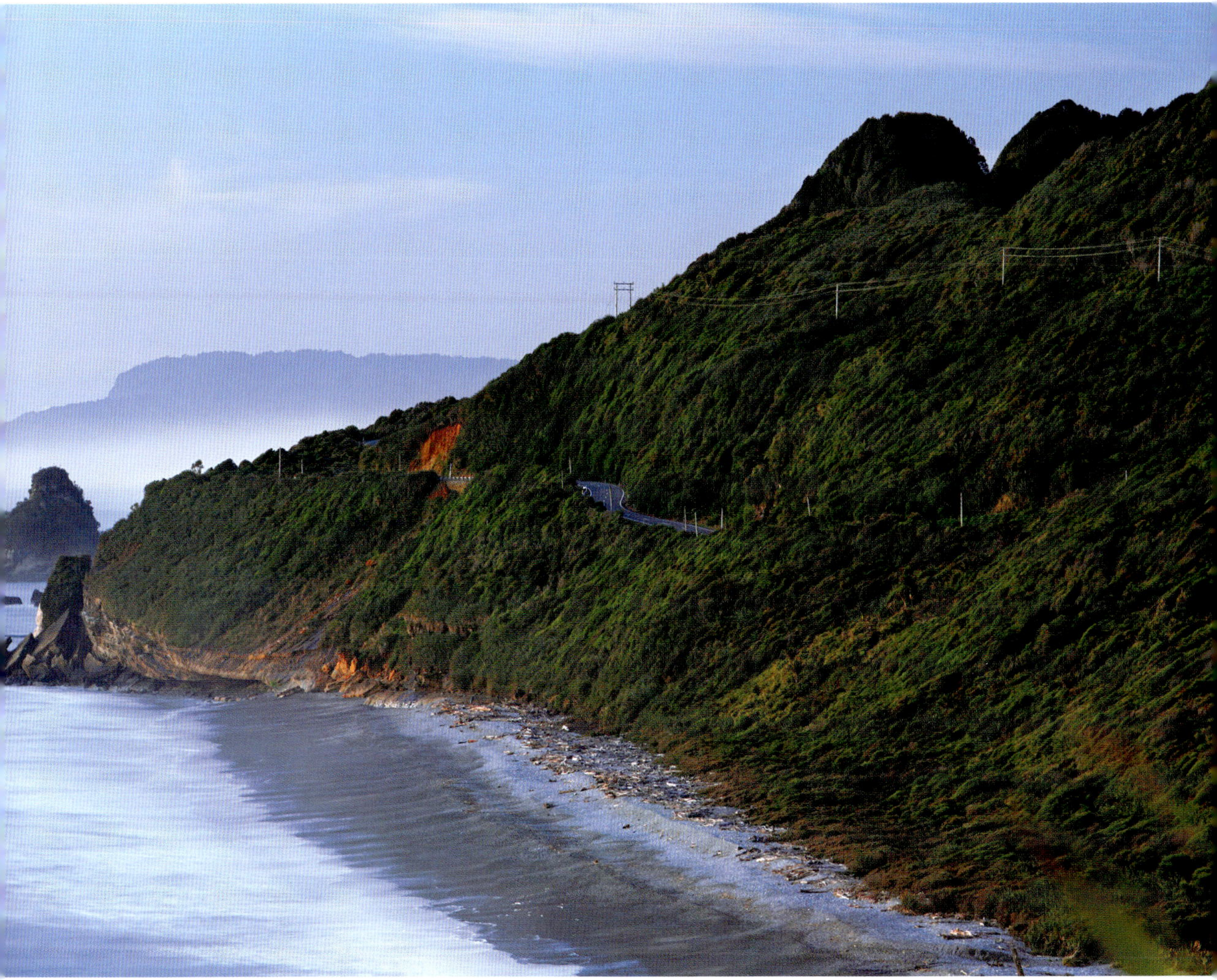

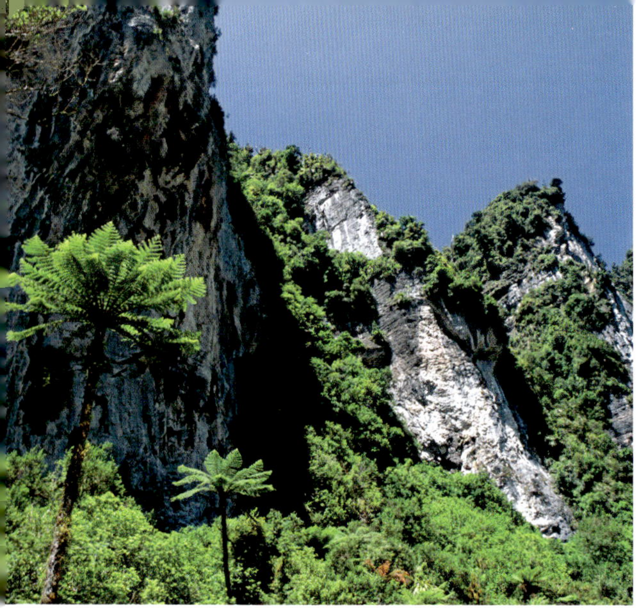

Previous pages: State Highway 6 finds a narrow route between the Paparoa Range and the sea near Motukiekie Rocks, north of Ten Mile Creek/ Waianiwaniwa.

Left: Limestone bluffs line the Fox River north of Punakaiki.

Below: Paparoa's moist and temperate climate has given rise to rich lowland forest, with native nikau palms providing a tropical ambience.

Right: The tranquil waters of Bullock Creek have worn a path through the soft limestone rocks.

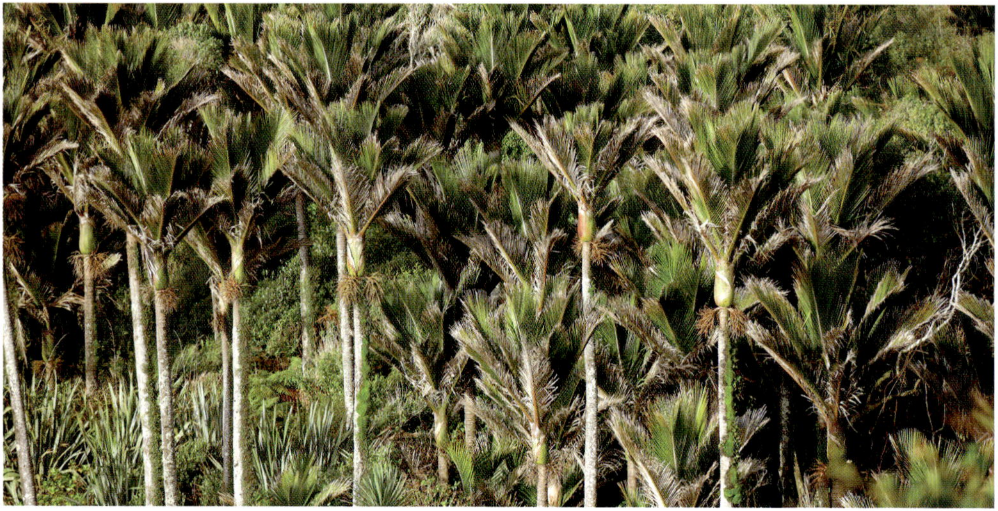

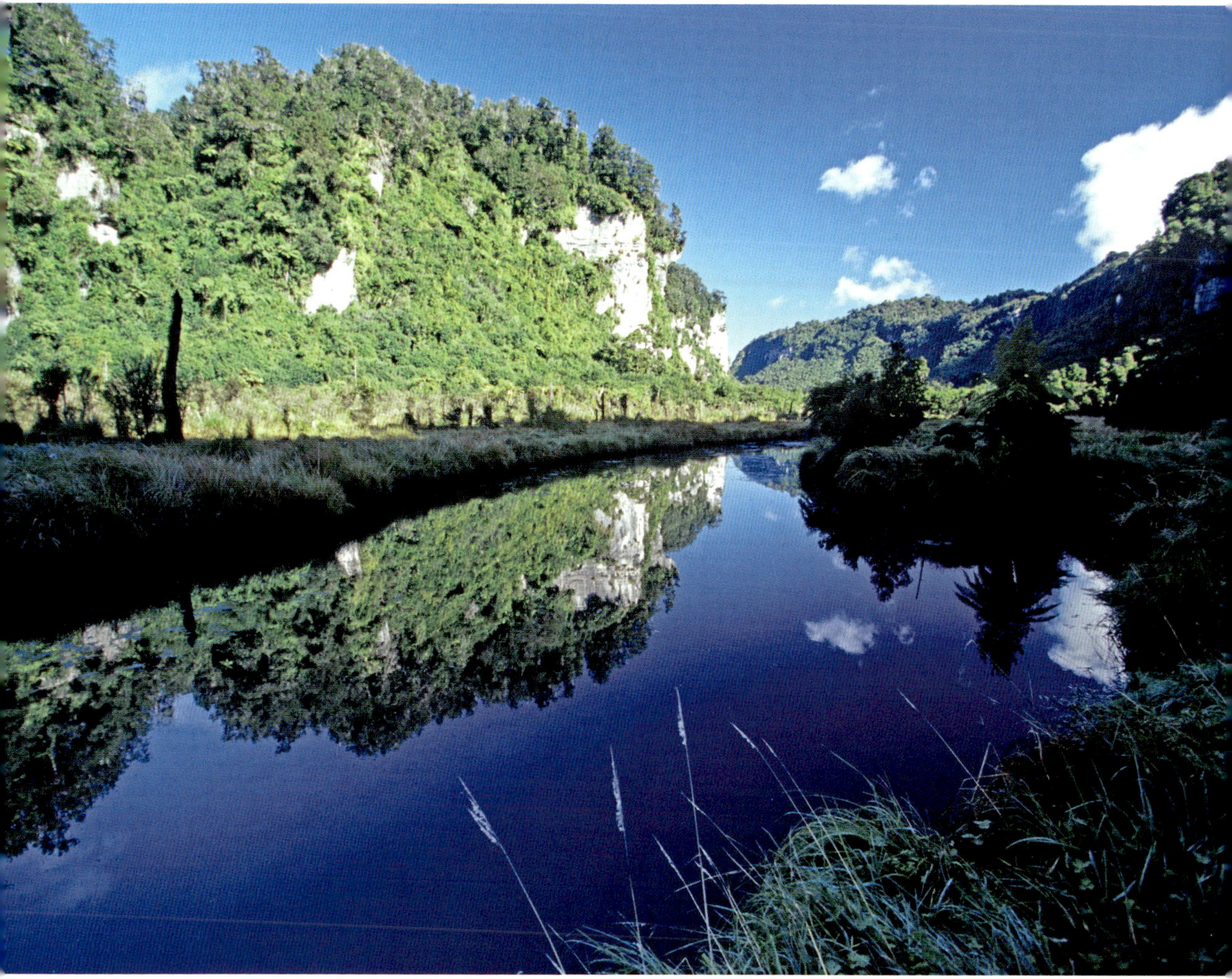

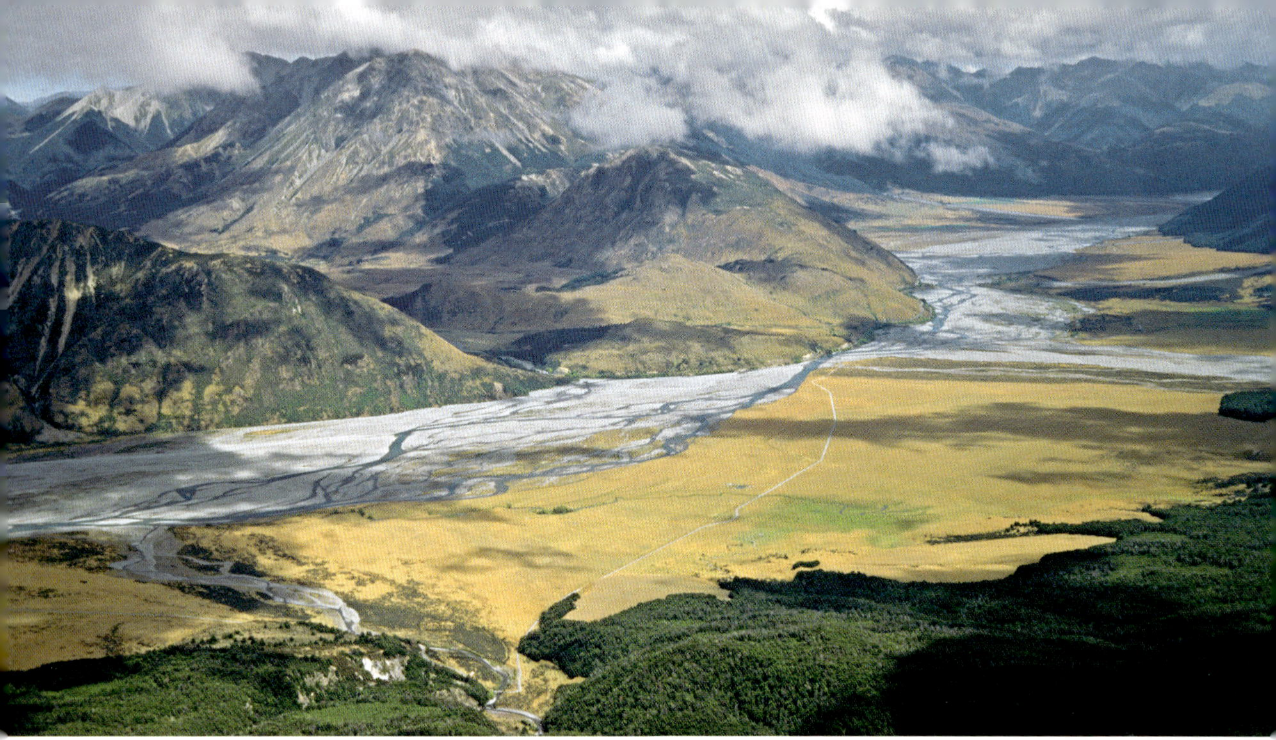

ARTHUR'S PASS

Arthur's Pass National Park straddles the Main Divide of the Southern Alps, a mountainous no-man's land between the plains of Canterbury and the forests of the West Coast foothills. It is a park of variety and distinctive alpine flora and bird life, including kea and kiwi. Near the historic pass itself craggy peaks of brittle greywacke, snowcapped for much or all of the year, offer grand panoramas. On the dry eastern slopes braided rivers run down long valleys while in the rain-soaked west the water tumbles to the sea through steep gorges and luxuriant rainforest. These contrasts make the park an endlessly intriguing playground for walkers, climbers and nature lovers.

Left: The braided Waimakariri River divides into a maze of channels as it heads east to the Pacific Ocean.

Right: A Mt Cook lily on Avalanche Peak. In the background is Mt Rolleston (2271 m), one of the highest peaks in the park.

Below: A steep climb up Lower Farm Stream into the mountains leads to a view over Castle Hill (right) and the head of Andrews Stream.

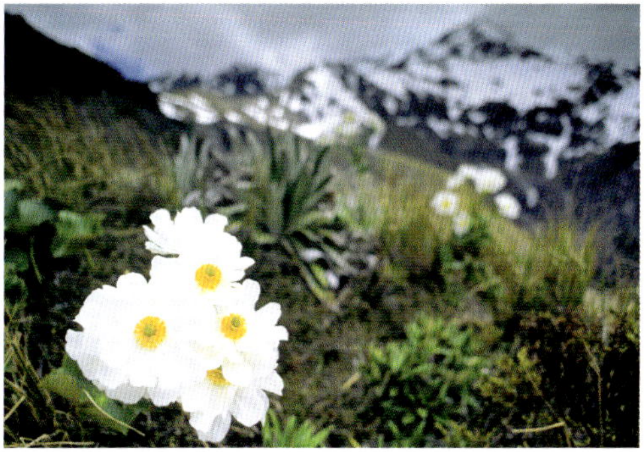

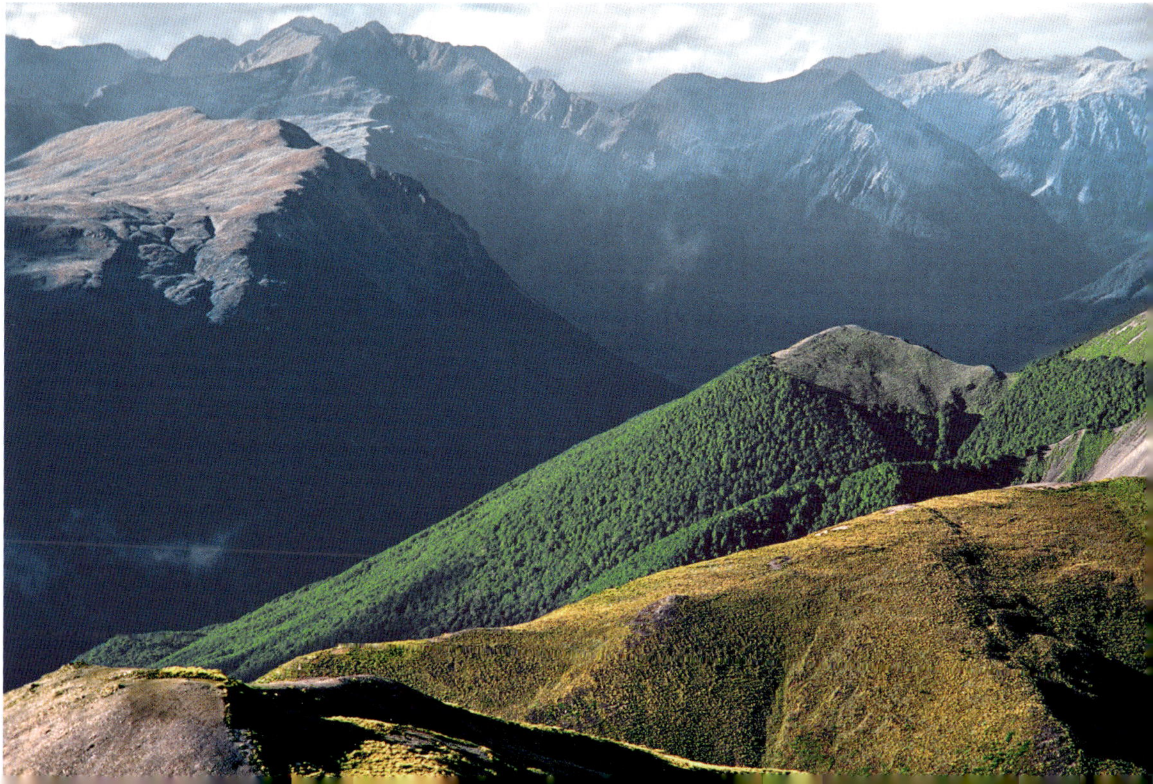

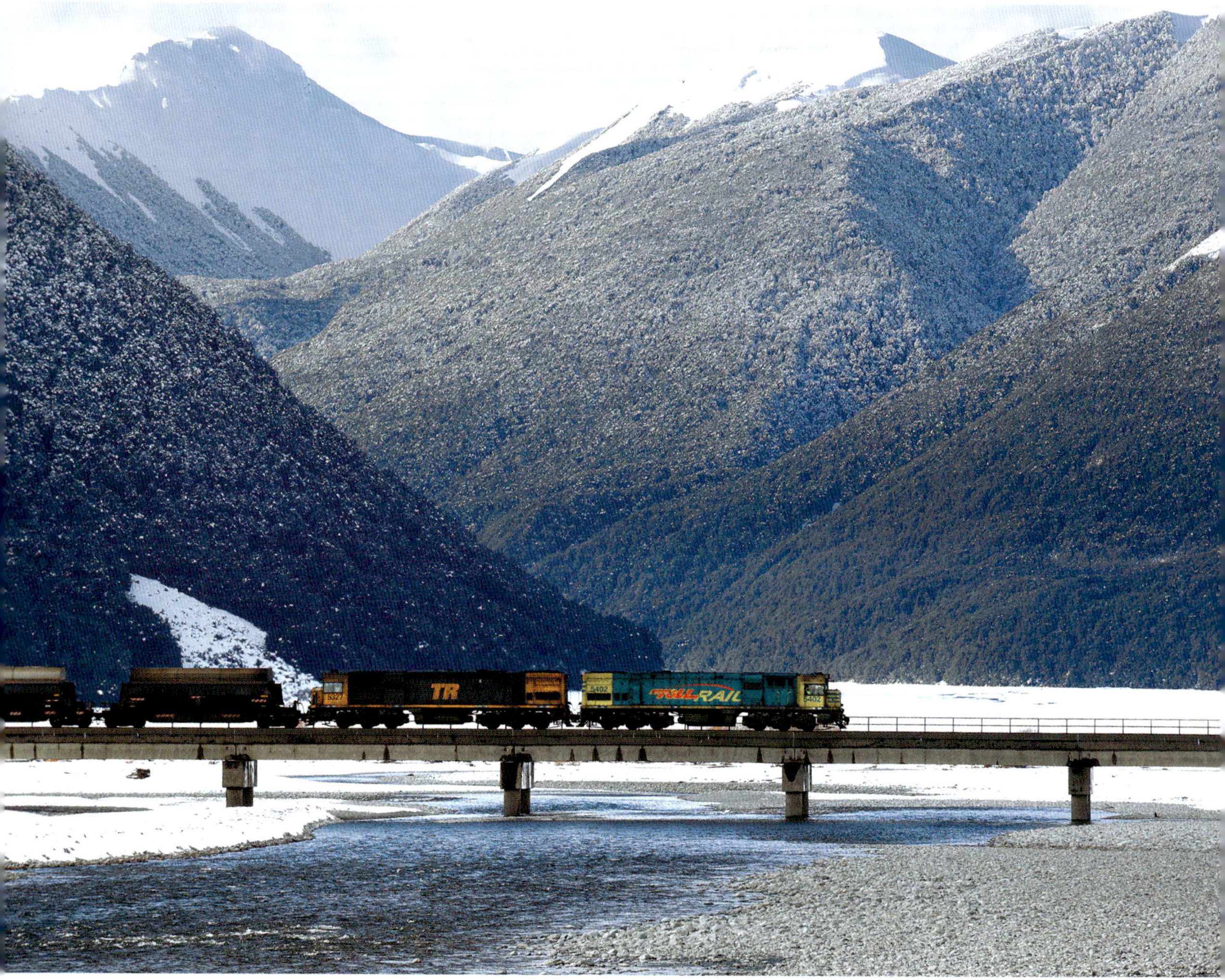
TR
TOLLRAIL

Left: A train carrying coal from the West Coast crosses the gravel bed of the Waimakariri River. The Hawdon Valley recedes into the distance.

Right: Kea play on the state highway at Arthur's Pass township. Tucked in a high-altitude valley between two massive ranges, the settlement is often beset by blizzards.

Below: The snow-capped peaks of the Southern Alps surround the Waimakariri's broad shingle bed.

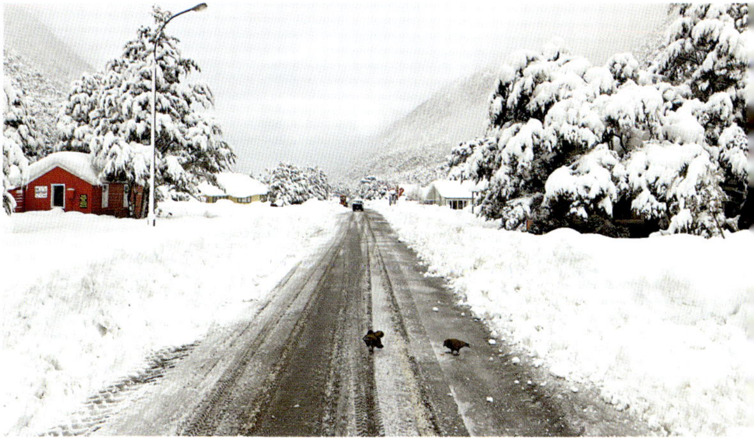

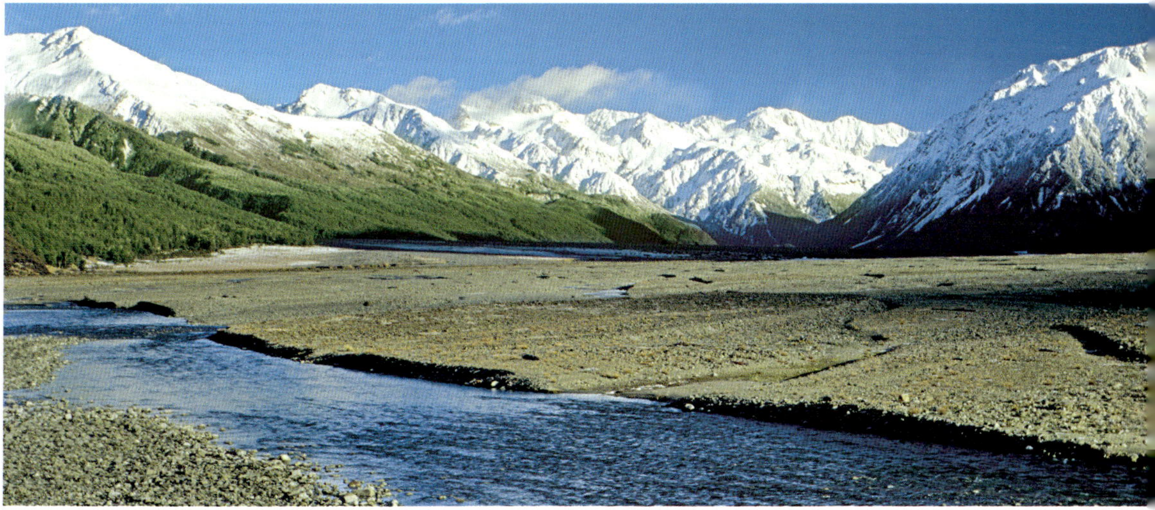

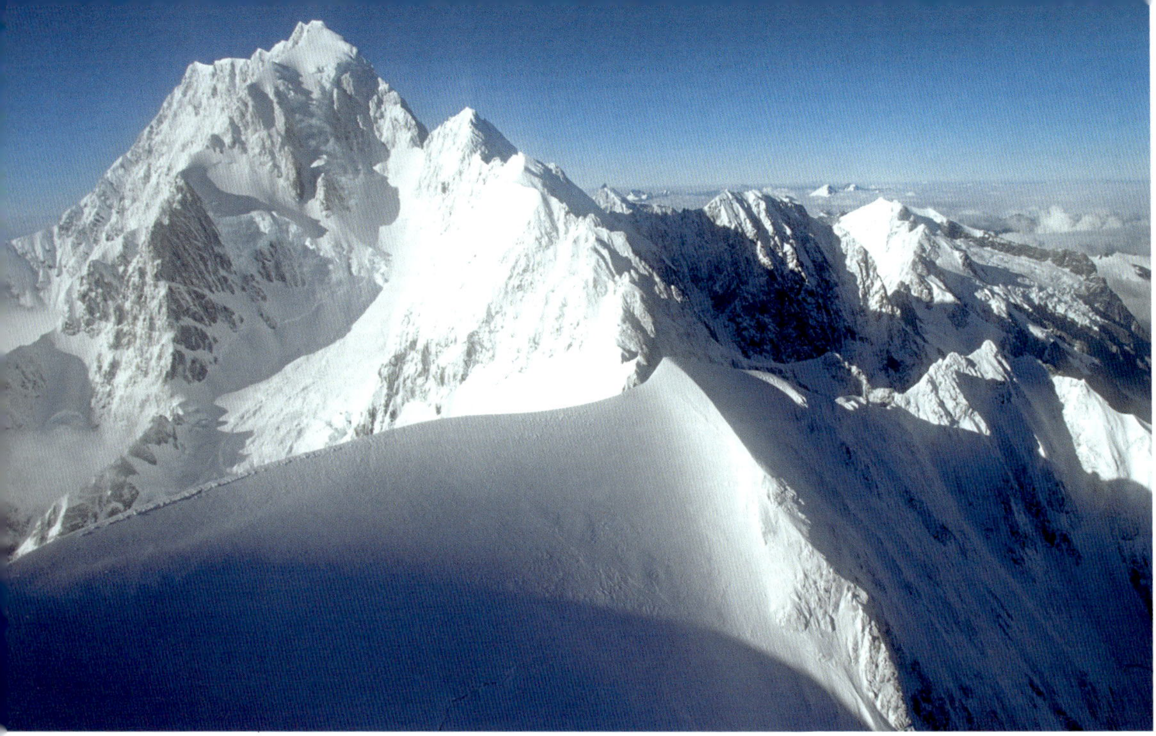

AORAKI/MT COOK

Aoraki/Mt Cook stands head and shoulders above New Zealand's other national parks. It's not just because it is the one at the highest altitude. The park is one of superlatives. It has the country's 20 highest peaks, as well as its biggest glaciers and most extensive snowfields. Mountaineers testify that this forbidding landscape of rock, snow and ice offers the best climbing in New Zealand and Australia, and skiers rave about the wide open slopes of the Tasman Glacier. Less intrepid visitors can absorb the grandeur from among the alpine flowers of the valleys or listen to the booming sounds of ice fall from the village of Mt Cook. The park is an integral part of the Te Waipounamu South Westland World Heritage Area.

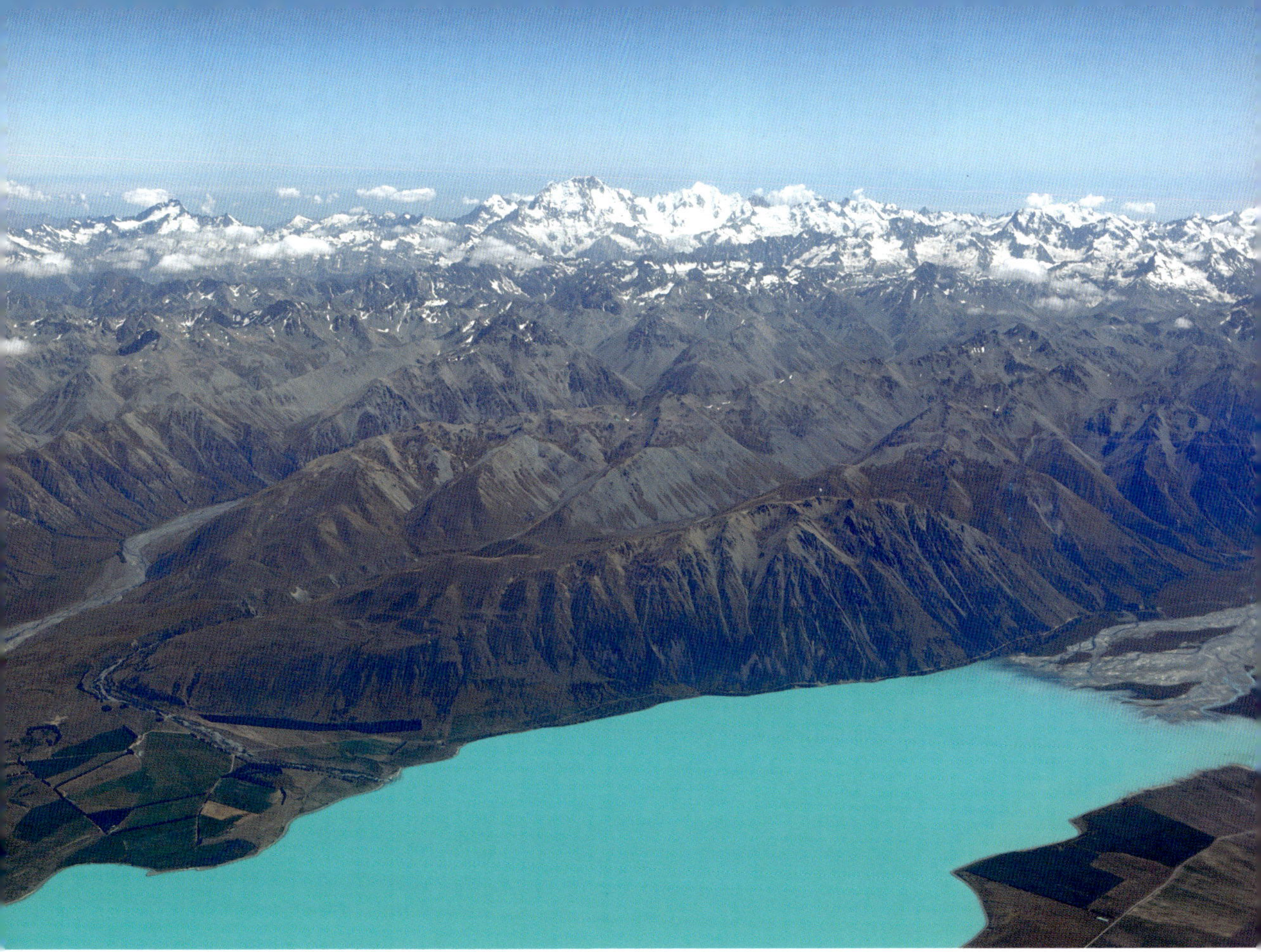

Left: Aoraki/Mt Cook (3754 m) is the highest mountain in New Zealand. Its perilous summit was first reached in 1894 by Tom Fyfe, Jack Clarke and George Graham.

Above: Aoraki/Mt Cook viewed from over Lake Tekapo in the Mackenzie Country, to the south-east of the national park. Taking a scenic flight is one way to appreciate the grandeur of the high peaks and the remarkable blue lakes, caused by the glacial rock flour.

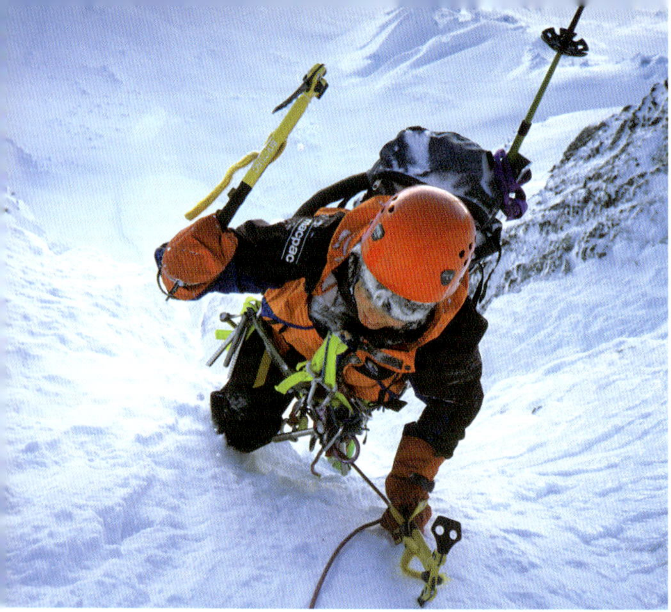

Left: Climbing Vampire (2645 m), a peak at the head of the Mueller Glacier, is a serious undertaking that requires skill, experience and technical climbing equipment.

Below: At Mt Cook Village a statue of Sir Edmund Hillary looks out over the mountains that were his training ground for Everest.

Right: Aoraki/Mt Cook, seen here from a mountaineer's perspective to the north, looks different from every angle and in every season.

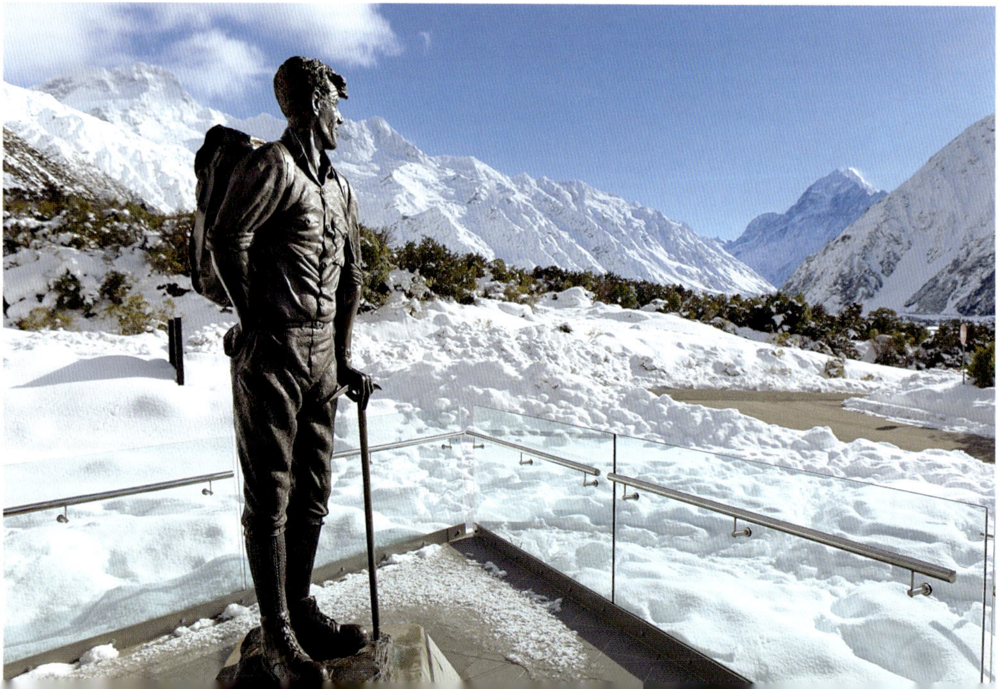

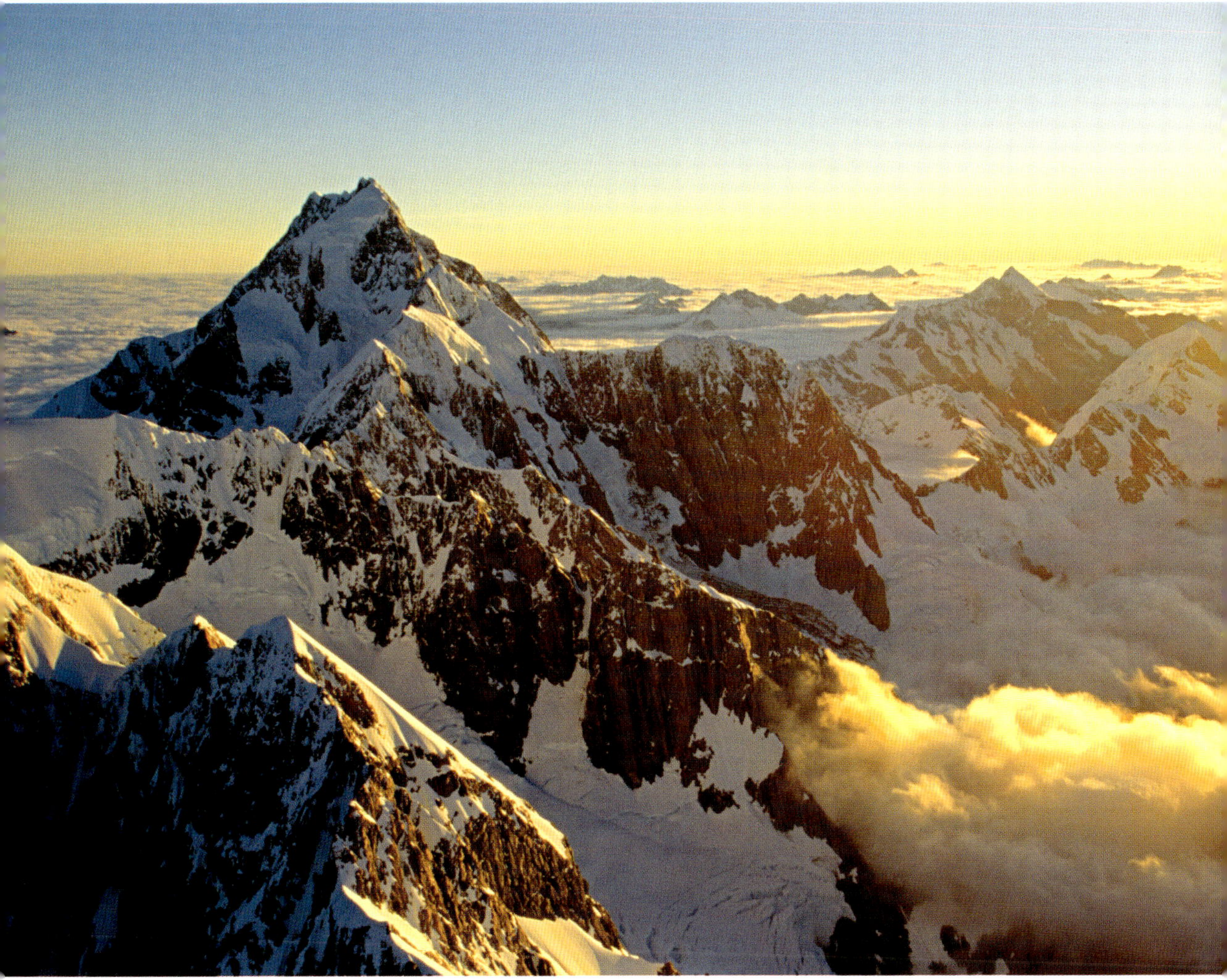

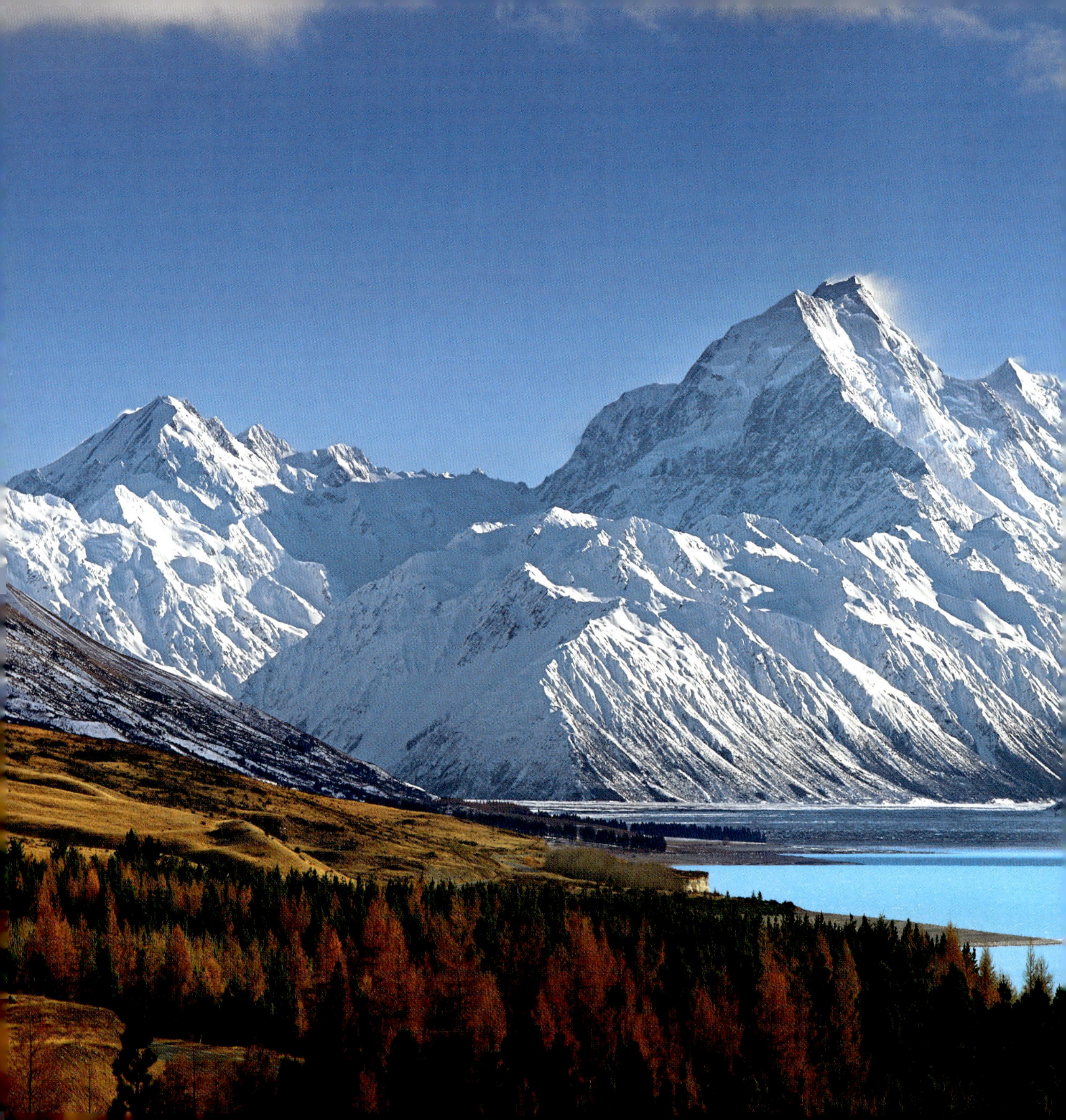

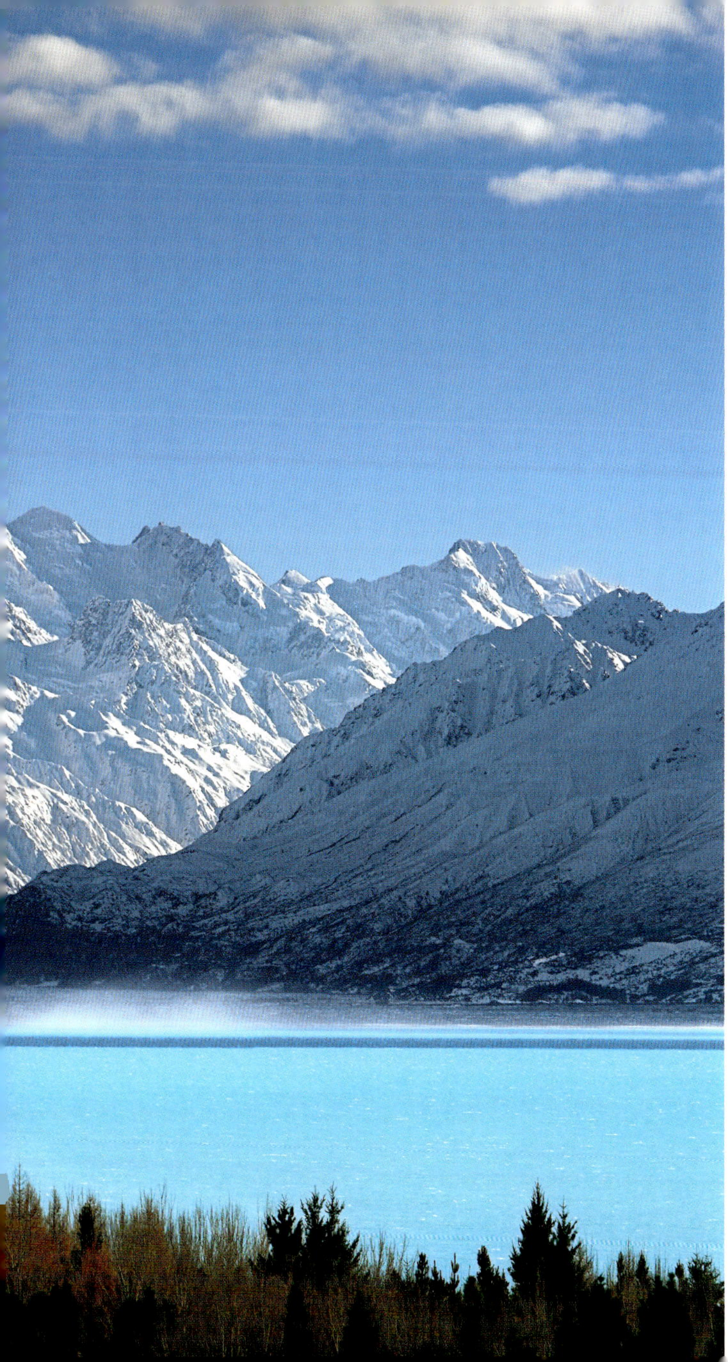

Left: Aoraki/Mt Cook soars above the chilly waters of Lake Pukaki. The lake's distinctive milky blue colour comes from finely ground rock deposited by the glaciers that feed it.

Below: The black-fronted tern/tarapiroe is one of several rare and unusual birds in the park.

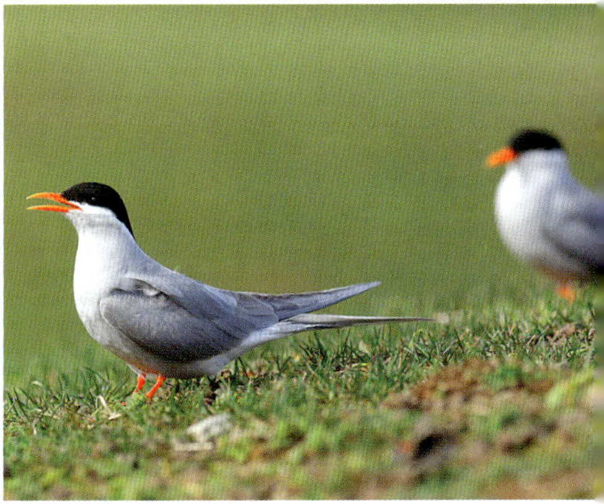

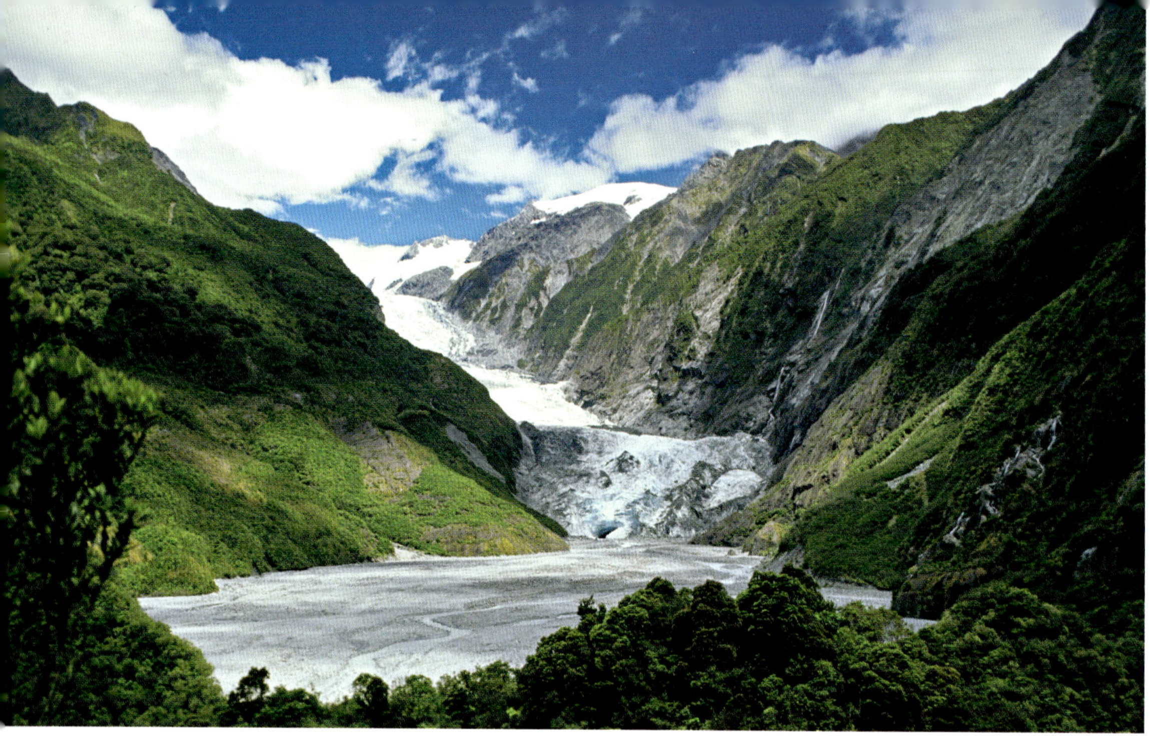

WESTLAND TAI POUTINI

Westland Tai Poutini National Park is neatly divided by the Alpine Fault that runs through its centre. To the south-east Earth's ever-shifting plates have forced the colossal mountains of the Southern Alps skyward, while to the north-west lowland plains run gently along the coastline. Two fast-moving glaciers, Fox and Franz Josef, link these very different sectors. They plunge down the precipitous mountainsides through a wilderness of temperate rainforests, tussock grasslands, lakes and lagoons towards the sea. Wading birds, some of them threatened, find a happy home in wetlands near the coast, while New Zealand's rarest kiwi snuffles around in the forests and kea haunt the alpine areas. For most, though, the main drawcards of the park are the two great glaciers.

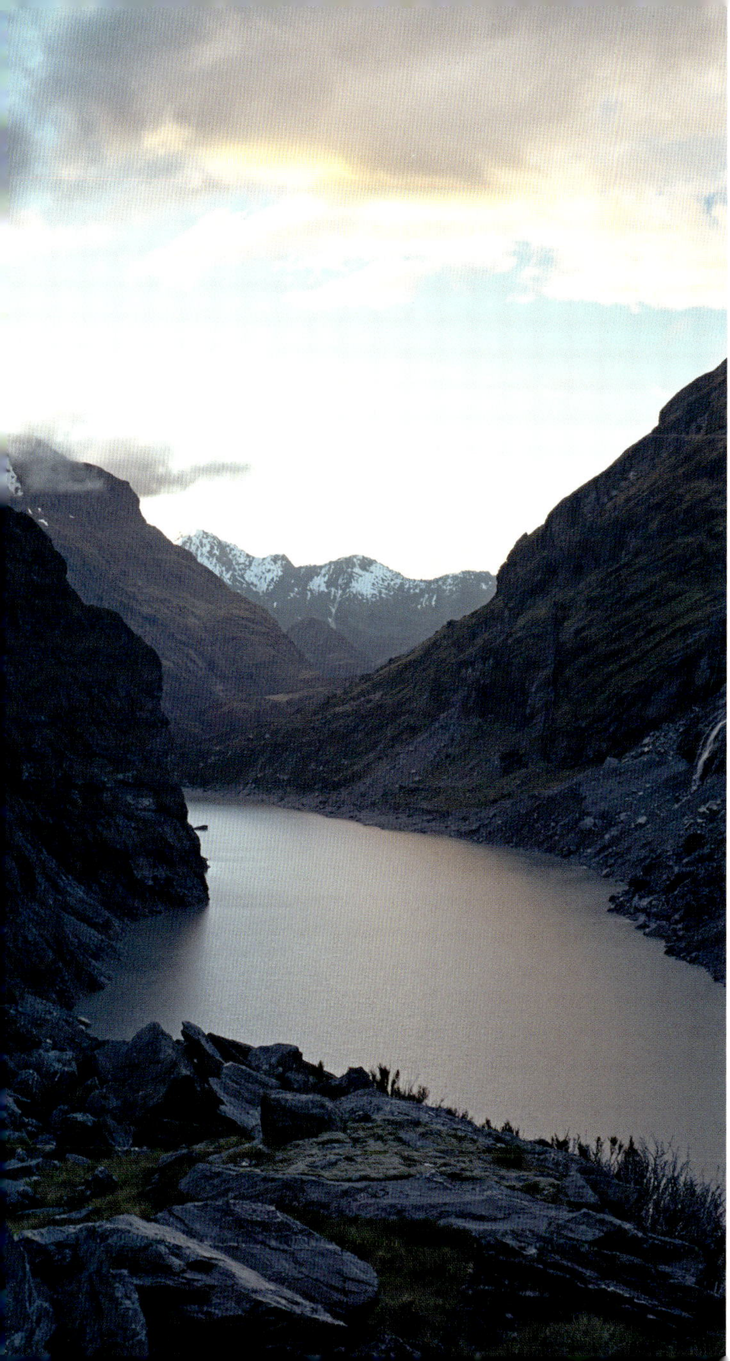

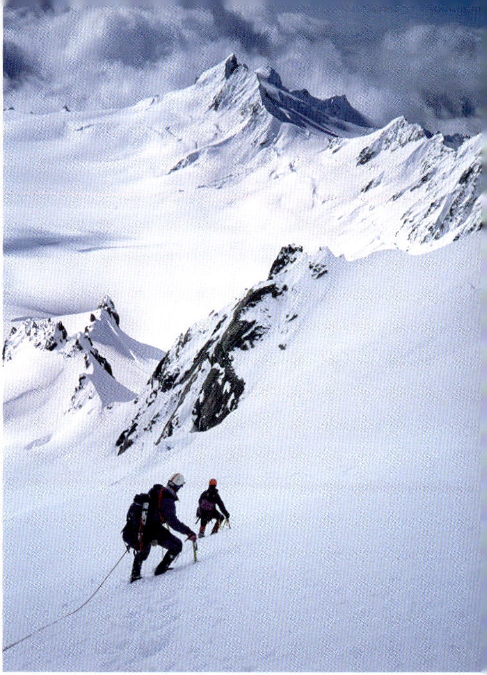

Far left: Franz Josef Glacier takes a steep course through a narrow valley from the Southern Alps down to rainforests near the coast.

Left: High in the mountains, Lake Douglas is the terminal lake of the Douglas Glacier, named after legendary surveyor Charlie Douglas; today, few adventurers visit this isolated spot.

Above: Mountaineers descending snowbound Douglas Peak are heading for the warmth and safety of Pioneer Hut.

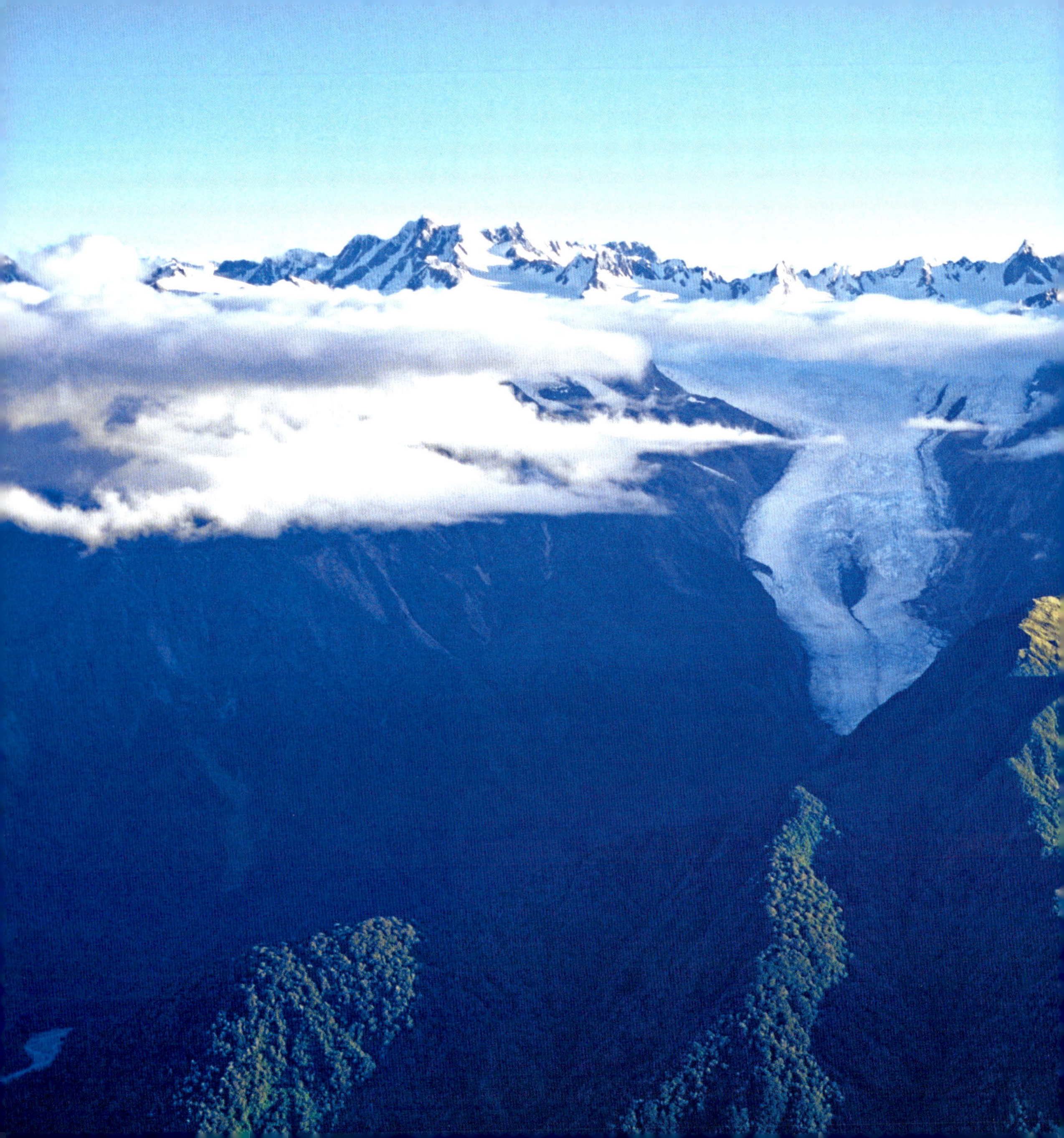

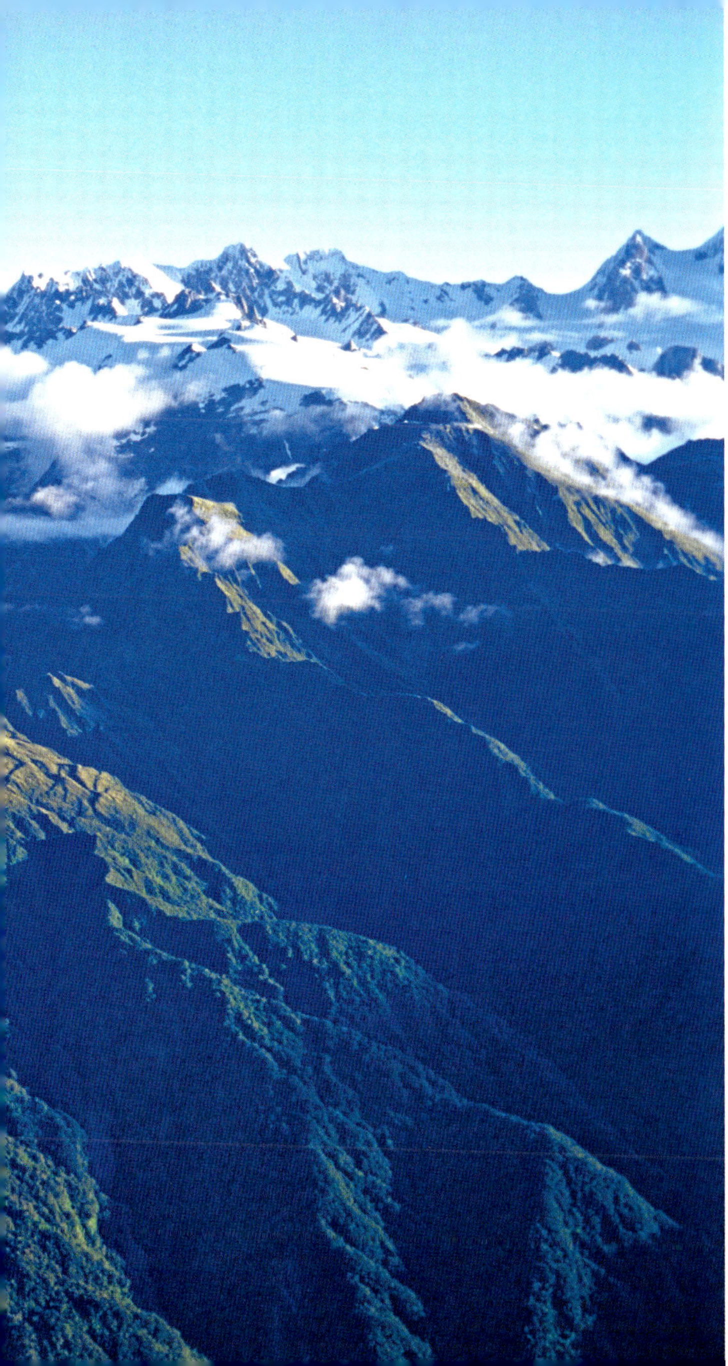

Left: Franz Josef Glacier is one of more than 60 glaciers in Westland Tai Poutini National Park, and one of the most accessible.

Below: Kahikatea, New Zealand's tallest tree, thrives in misty flax swamps near the coast.

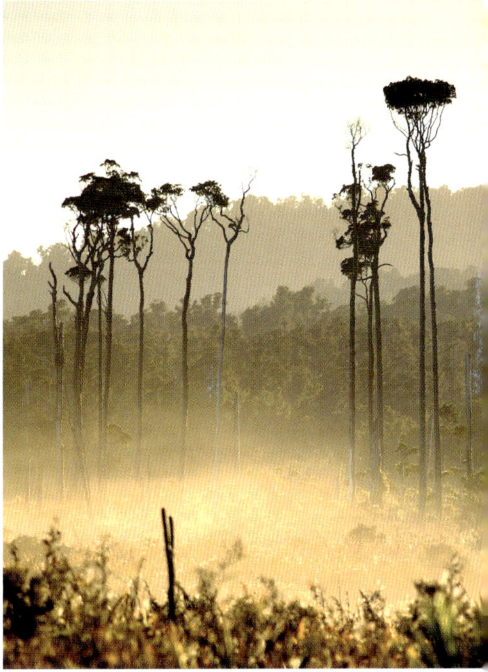

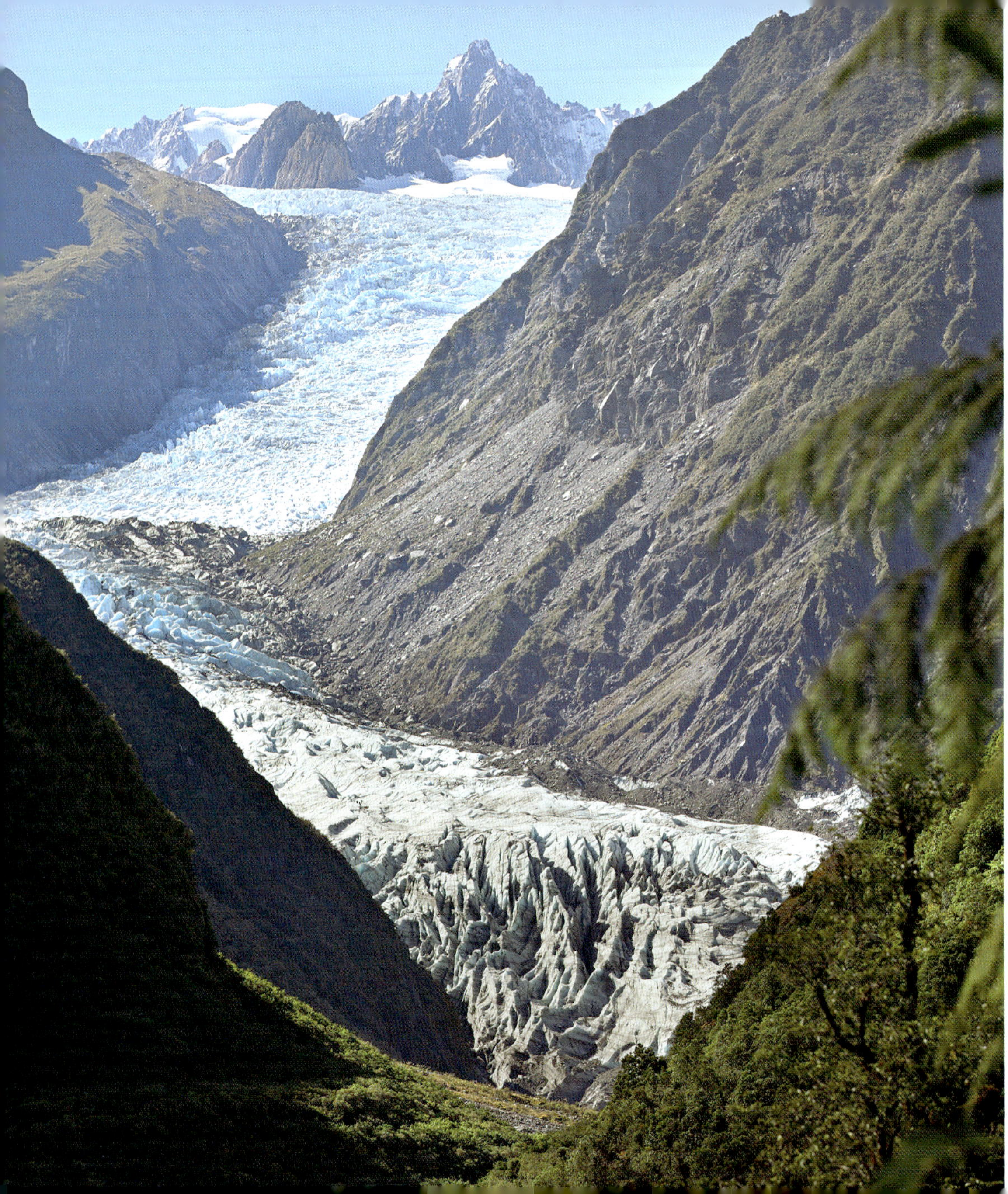

Left: The upper reaches of the fast-moving Fox Glacier are dominated by the rock pyramid of Douglas Peak (3077 m), seen in the centre distance.

Right: On a calm morning the waters of Lake Matheson mirror the panorama of the Southern Alps.

Below: The black sands of remote and wild Gillespies Beach were once mined for gold.

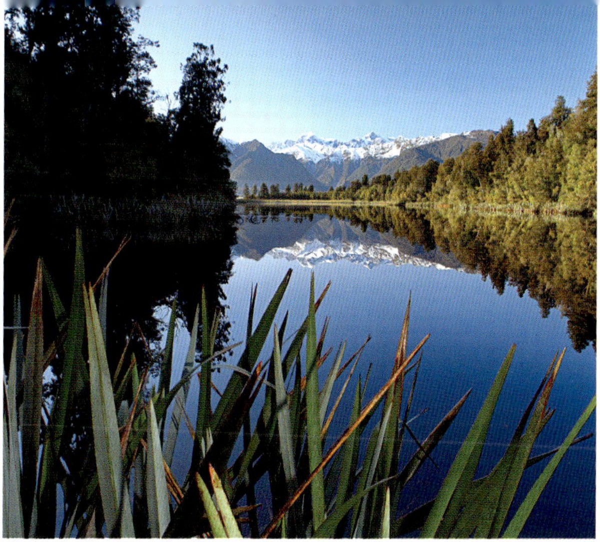

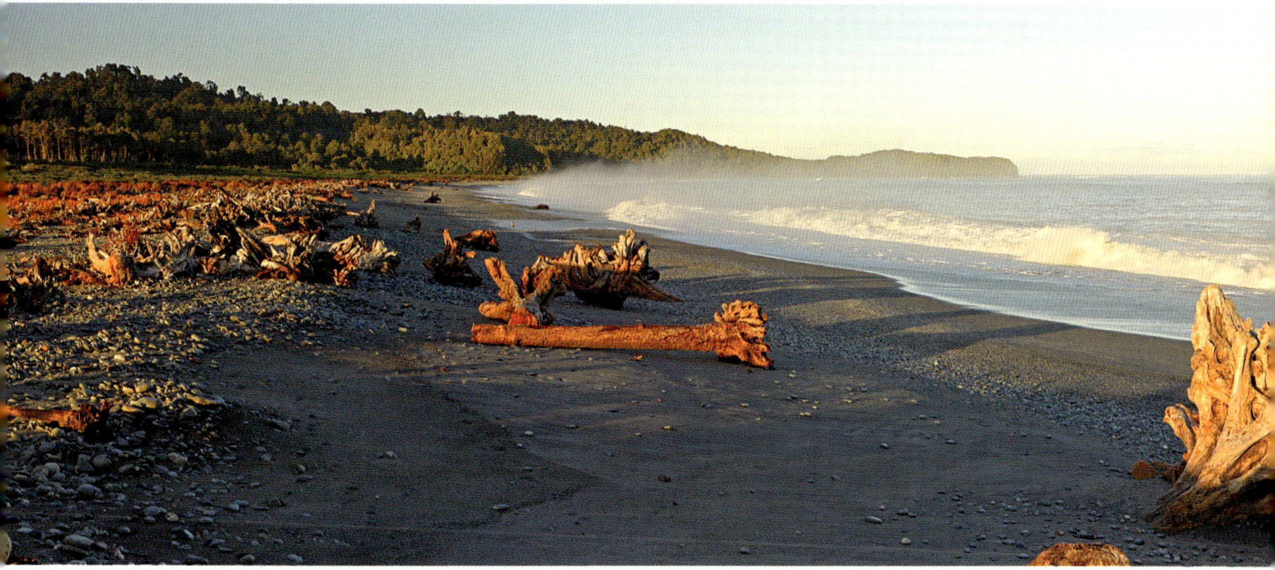

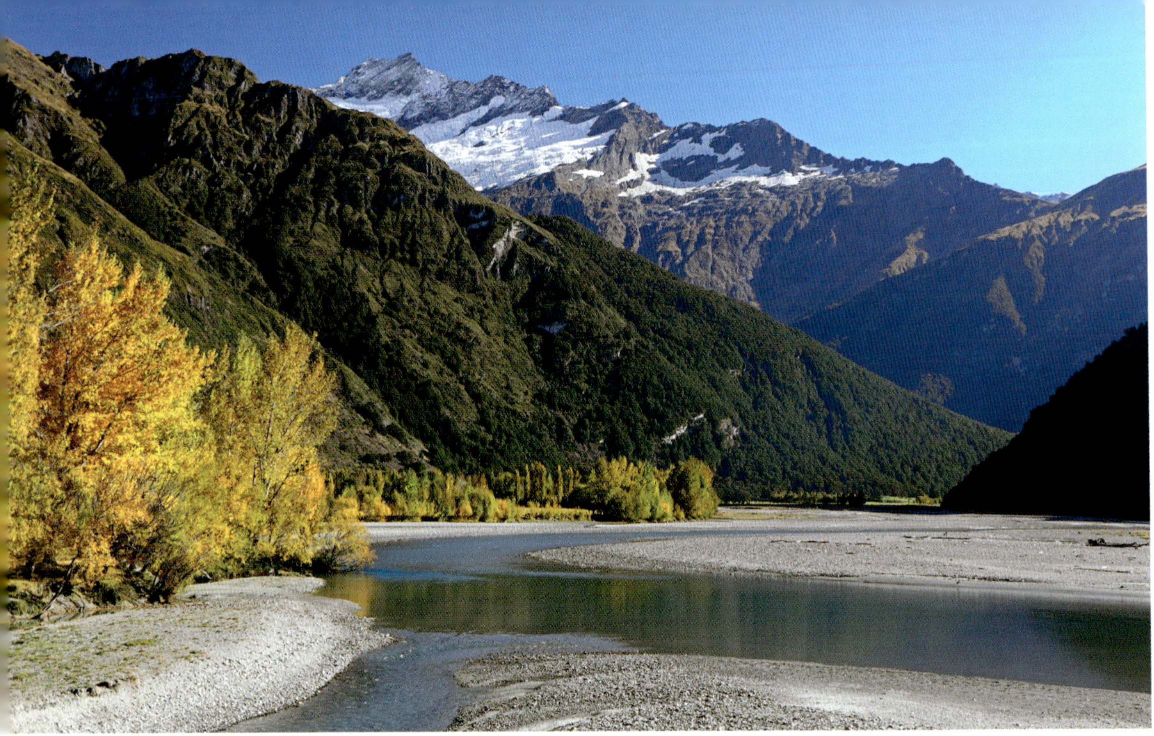

MT ASPIRING

Magnificent Mt Aspiring National Park is a mecca for mountaineers, hikers and amblers alike. The many rocky peaks are flanked by glaciers, permanent snowfields and an ice plateau, providing a challenge for the most experienced climbers. Whittled by glaciation into horns and teeth, they stand guard over frigid lakes and rivers, subalpine meadows, wide grassy valleys and unmodified beech forest. This is the habitat of tiny forest and mountain birds as well as the fearless and mischievous kea. The magnesium-rich Red Hills, in contrast, are almost completely barren. Parts of the large park are rarely visited and are preserved as remote wilderness areas, while others, just as dramatic, are penetrated by well-travelled tracks. Wherever you go there are unforgettable vistas at every turn.

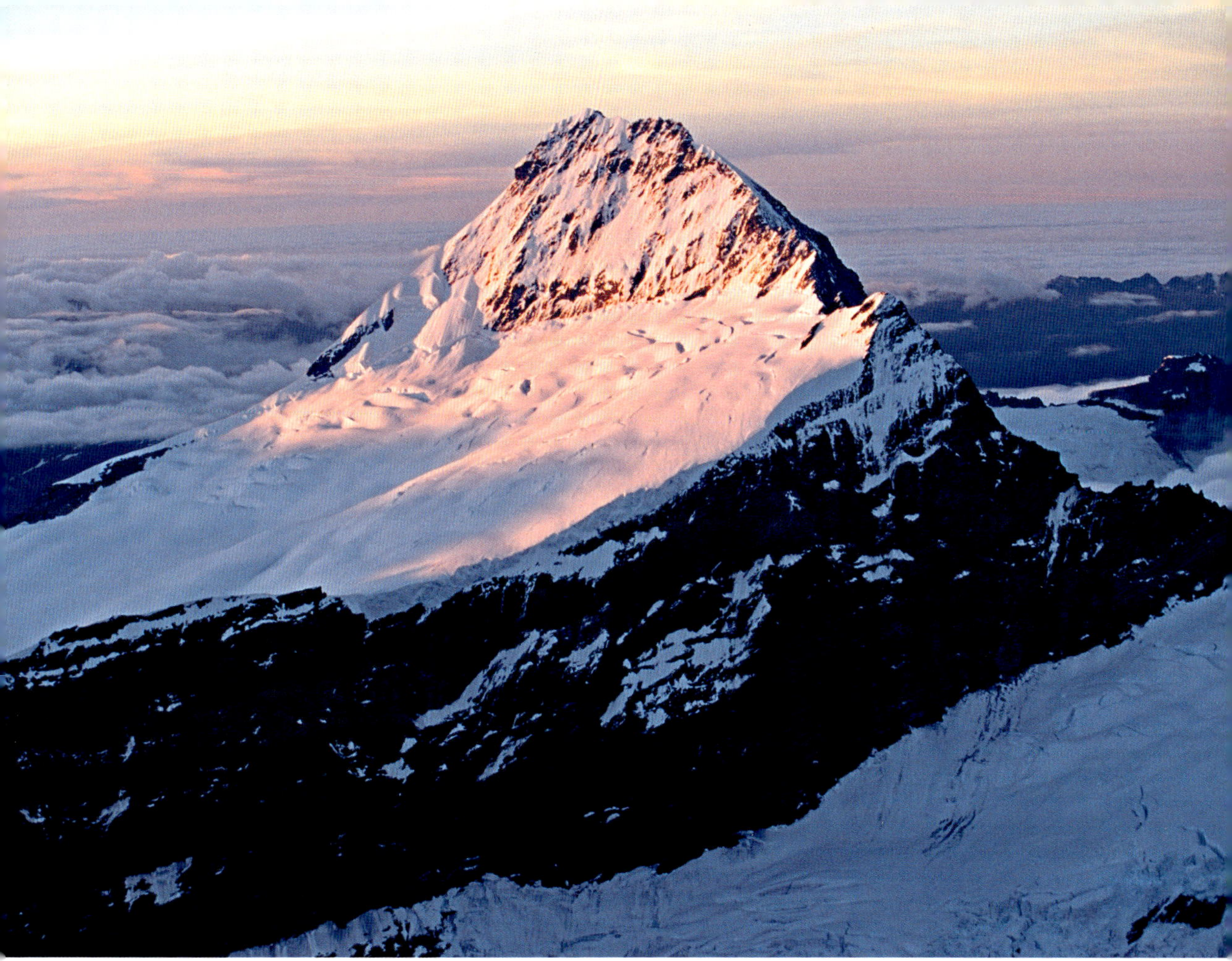

Left: In autumn, the exotic trees that line the Matukituki River below Mt Avalanche light up the landscape of Cameron Flat. Two branches of the Matukituki – the east and the west – flow into Mt Aspiring National Park.

Above: Mt Aspiring/Tititea (3033 m) is a sentinel towering above the mountains around it. It is the highest peak outside the Mt Cook area, and climbing it is a rite of passage for local mountaineers.

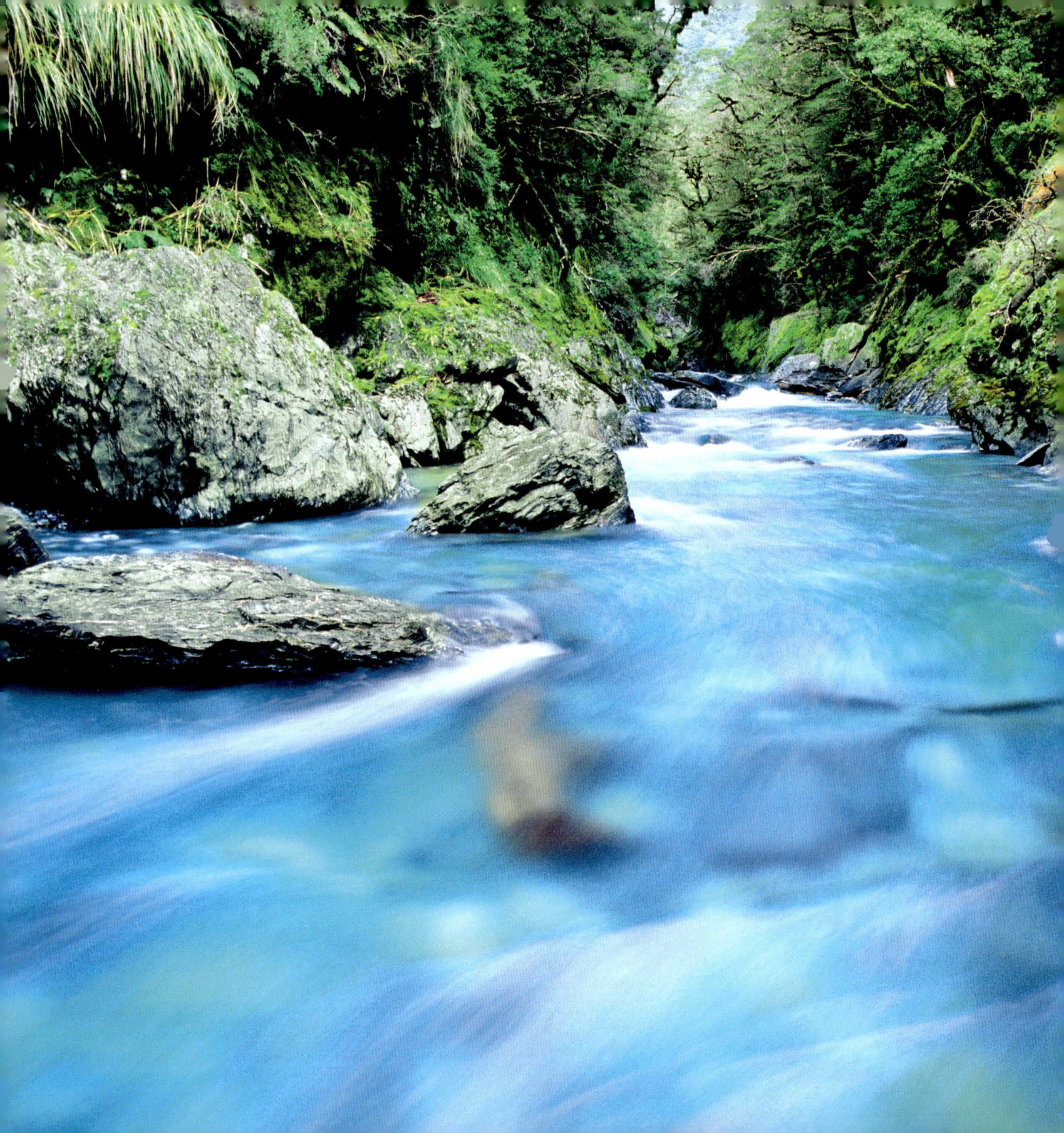

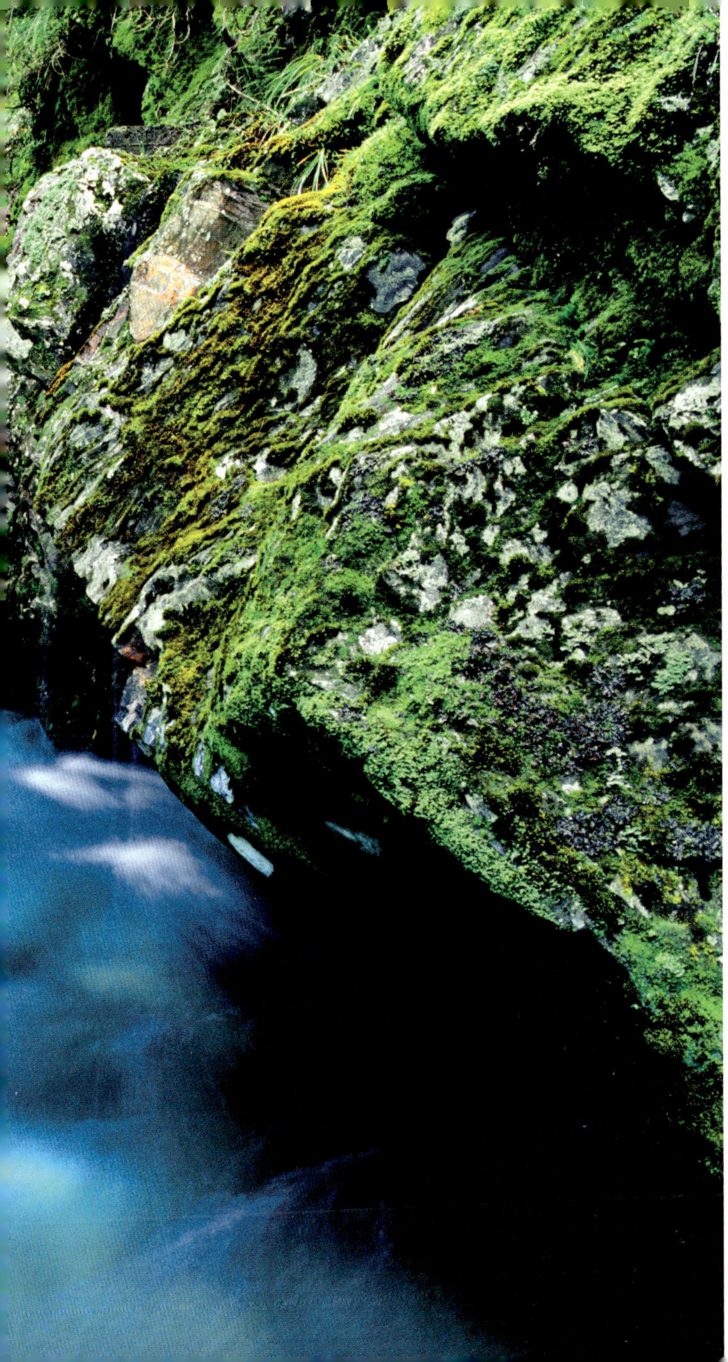

Left: The Fish River, a tributary of the Makorora River, runs swift and strong through the Haast Pass area, one of the rainiest places in New Zealand.

Below: The South Island robin, searching for invertebrates disturbed by boot-clad feet, is a frequent sight on walking tracks.

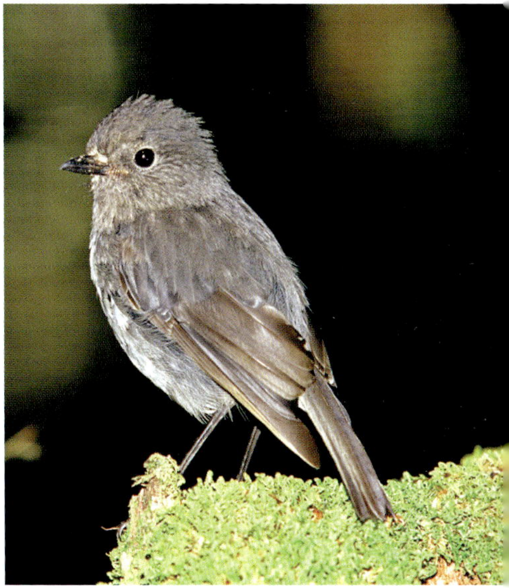

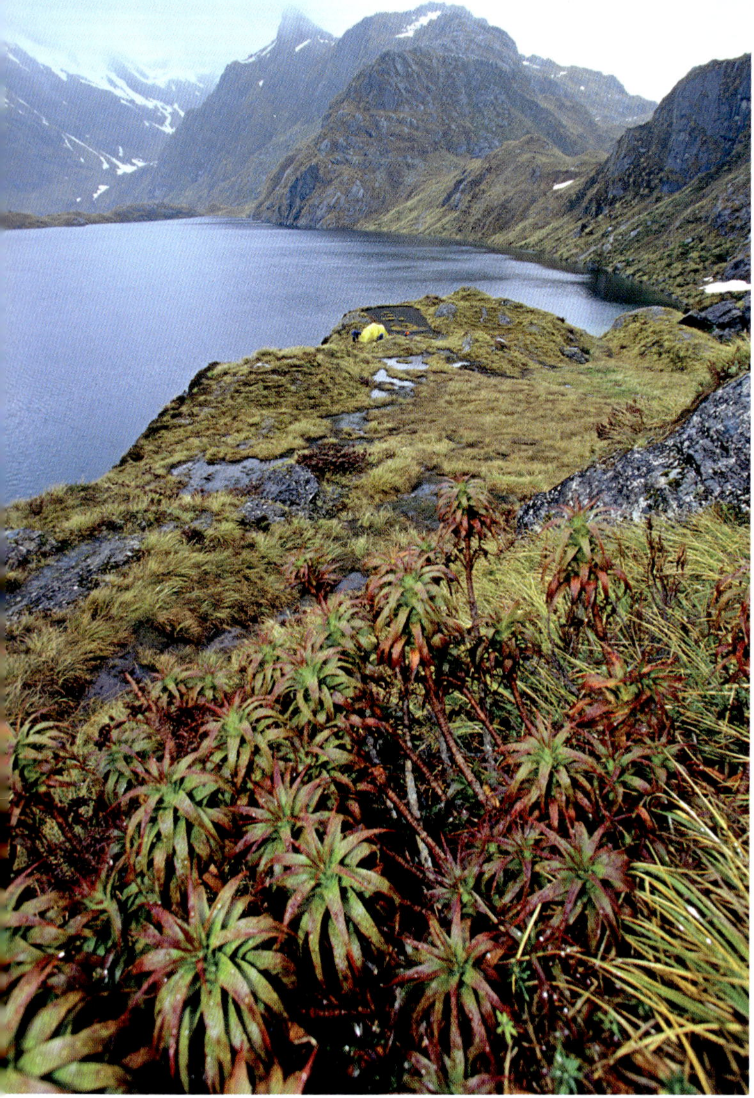

Left: An alpine lake in the Serpentine Range; the moisture-loving pineapple scrub in the foreground is doubtless enjoying the rain more than the camper on the shore.

Below: The Routeburn Track, with its well-maintained track and many bridged river crossings, is one of the most achievable of the Great Walks.

Right: A landslip on the Routeburn Track has opened up a grand view of Routeburn Flats and the Humboldt Mountains.

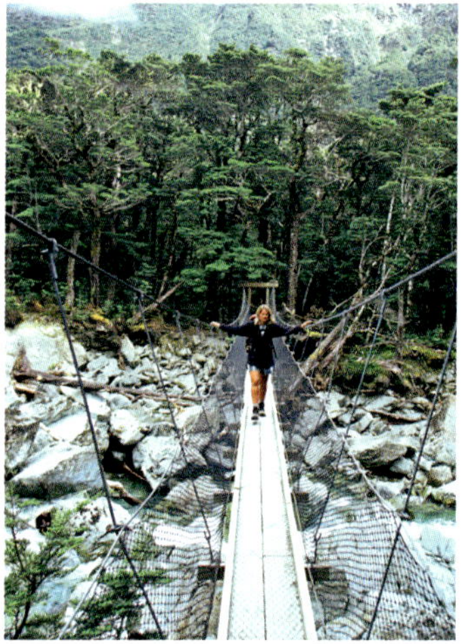

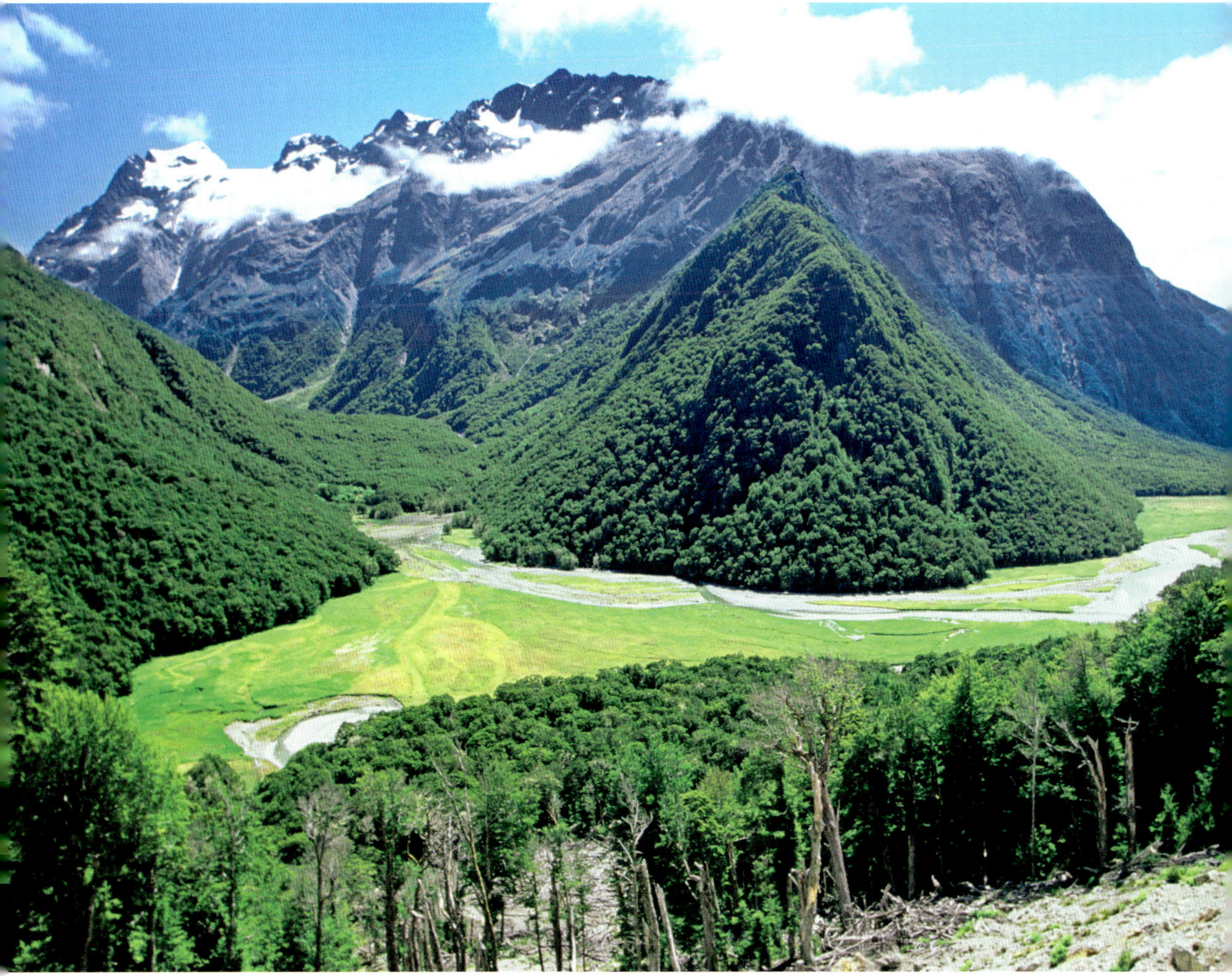

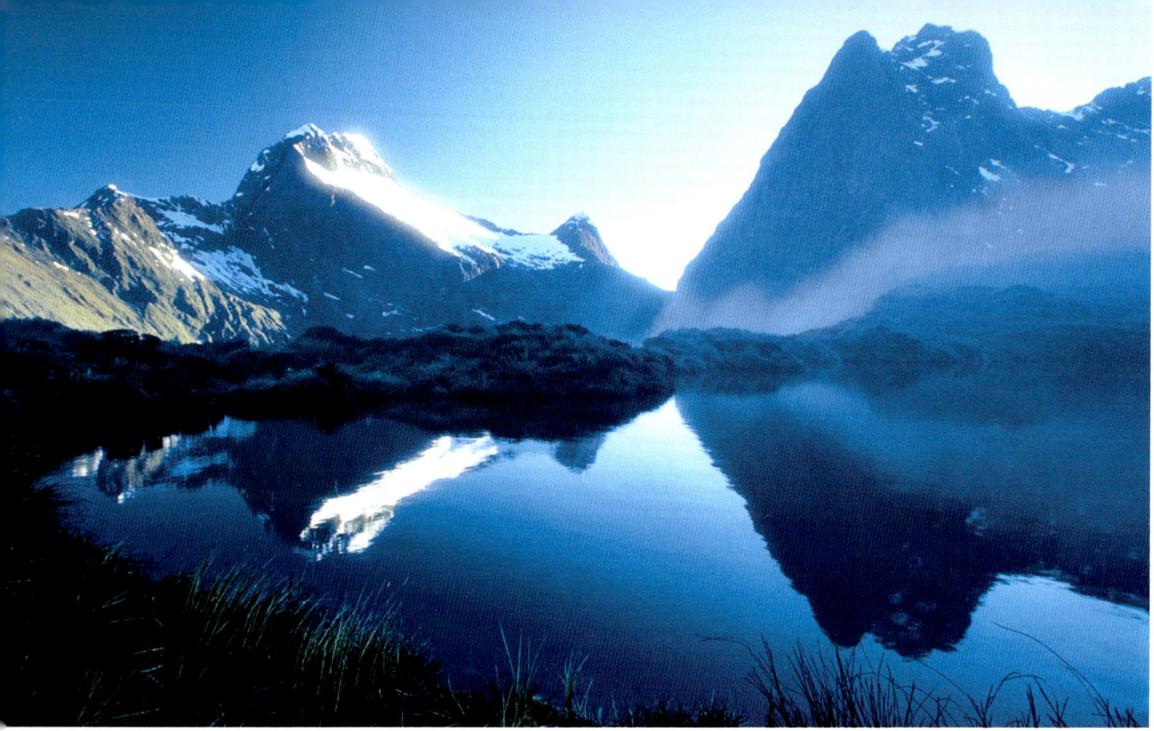

FIORDLAND

In the south-western corner of the South Island the vast expanse of Fiordland, with its glacier-carved mountains, inlets and lakes and its verdant beech forests and alpine meadows, is one of the finest wilderness areas in the world. A journey along the park's single highway and a cruise or a scenic flight offer more than enough breathtaking views of towering peaks, sheer valley walls and twinkling water to satisfy most visitors. But some energetic types find the only way to properly take in this dramatic place, to hear the bird song and see the rare and unusual plant life and experience the wild weather, is to travel one of the park's world-famous walking tracks, climb the mountains, kayak the fiords or camp under the stars.

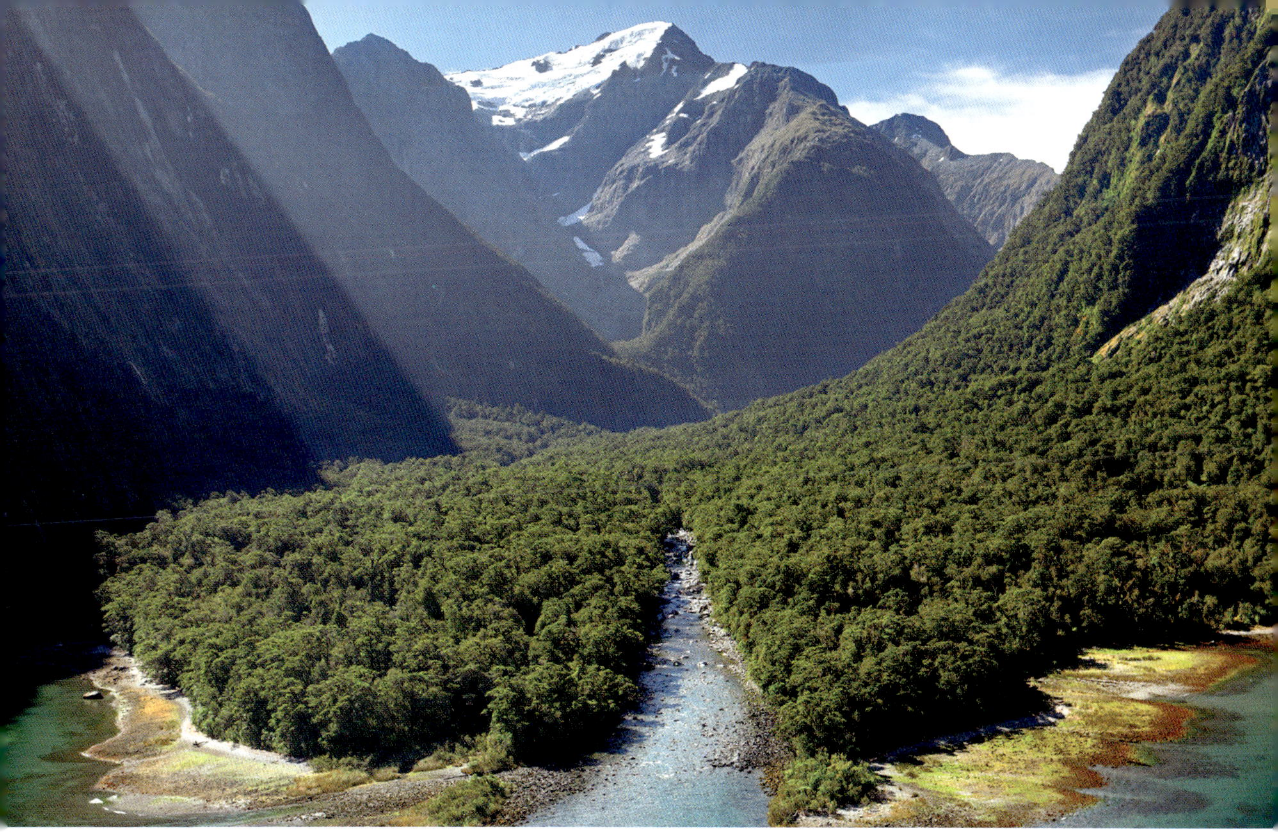

Left: Early morning mist veils the outlook from Mackinnon Pass on the Milford Track Great Walk. Mt Elliot and Mt Balloon dominate the skyline.

Above: The Harrison River flows through beech forest along the floor of a glacial valley and into Milford Sound.

Right: The rare Fiordland crested penguin breeds in dense coastal forests close to the shoreline of the sounds.

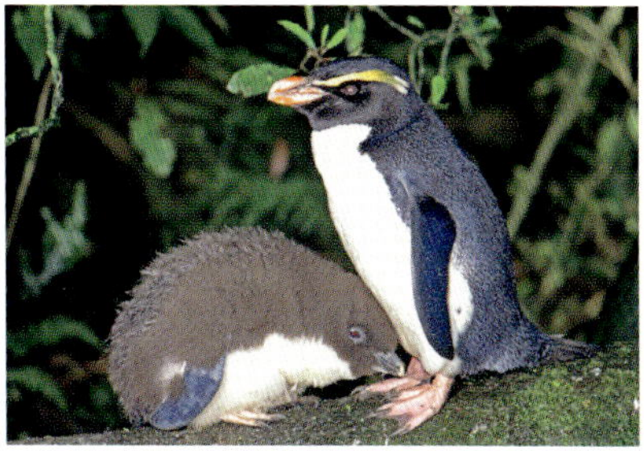

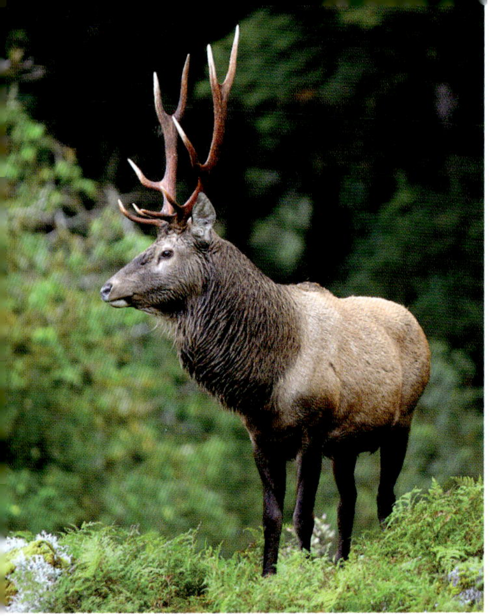

Left: In Fiordland, wapiti (elk), gifted to New Zealand by Teddy Roosevelt in 1905, have interbred with Scottish red deer to produce a hybrid. The large antlers of the wapiti make it a sought-after trophy for hunters.

Below: Giant Gate Falls in the Arthur River valley is one of many rushing waterfalls visible – especially after a good downpour – from the Milford Track Great Walk.

Right: Luxmore Hut, on the Kepler Track Great Walk, has a wonderful position overlooking Lake Te Anau and the Murchison Mountains.

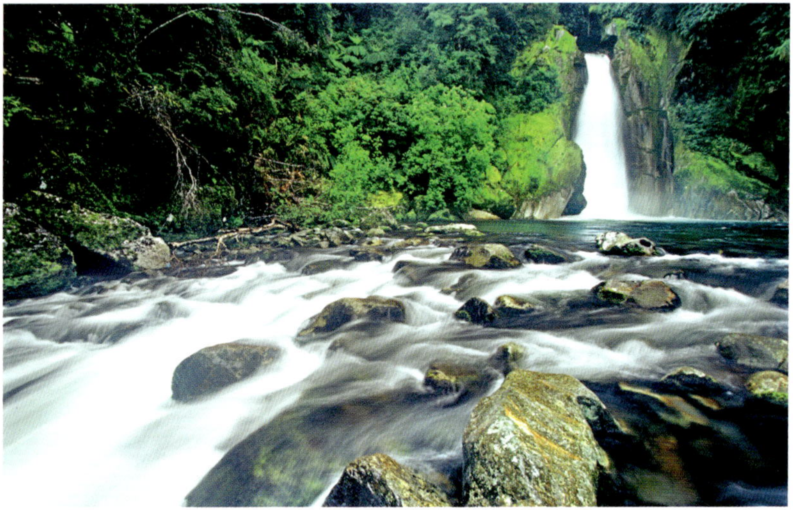

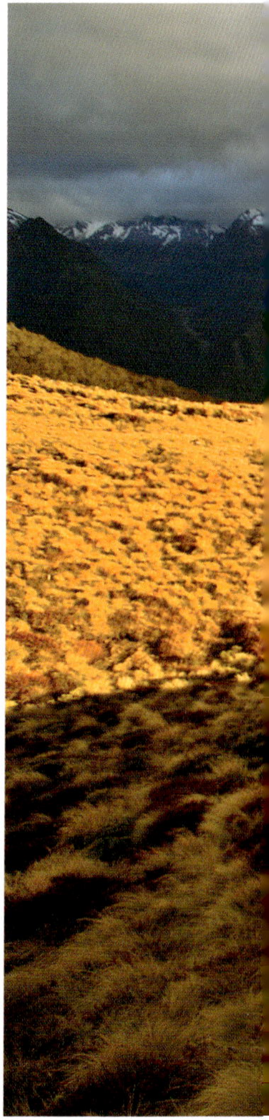

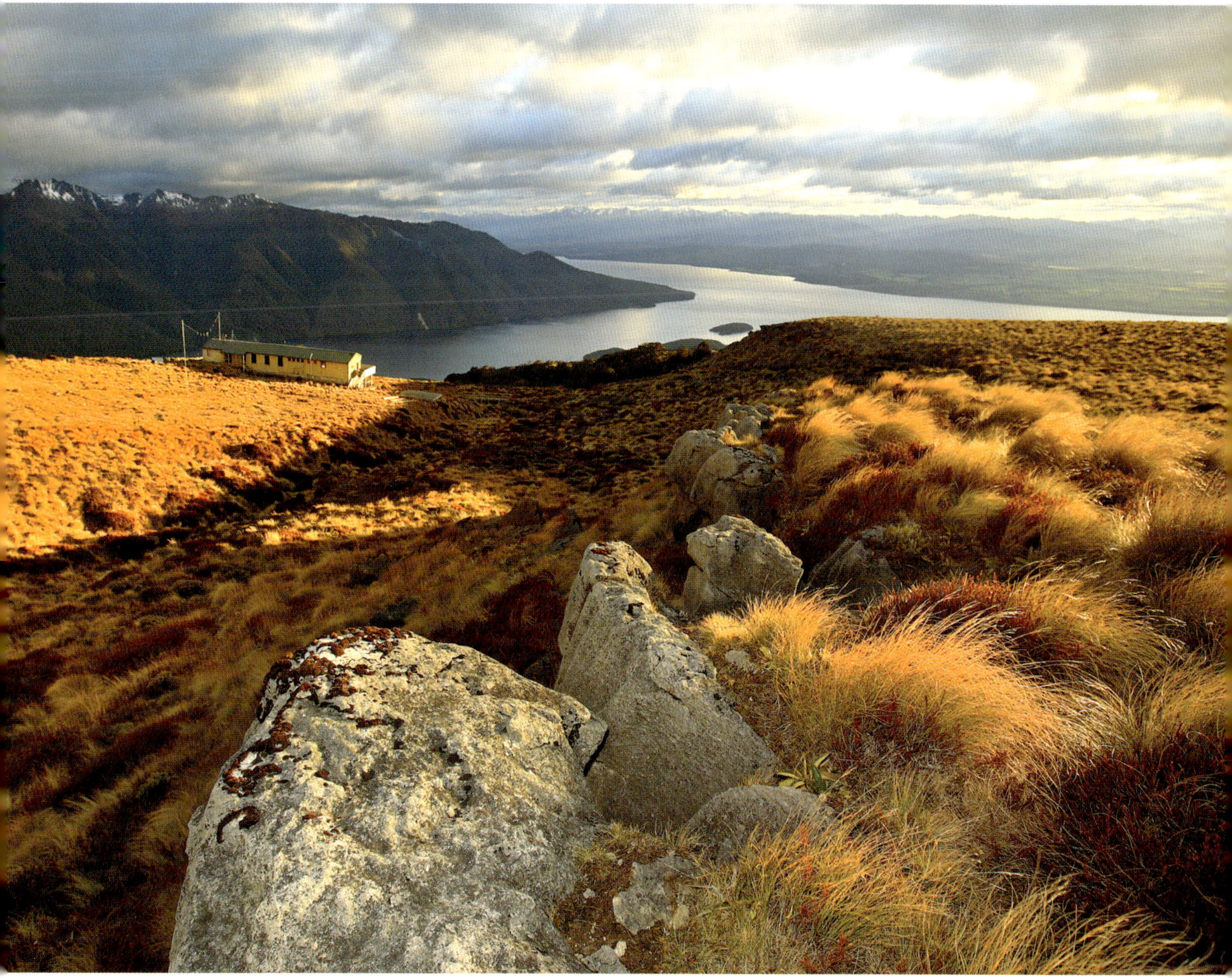

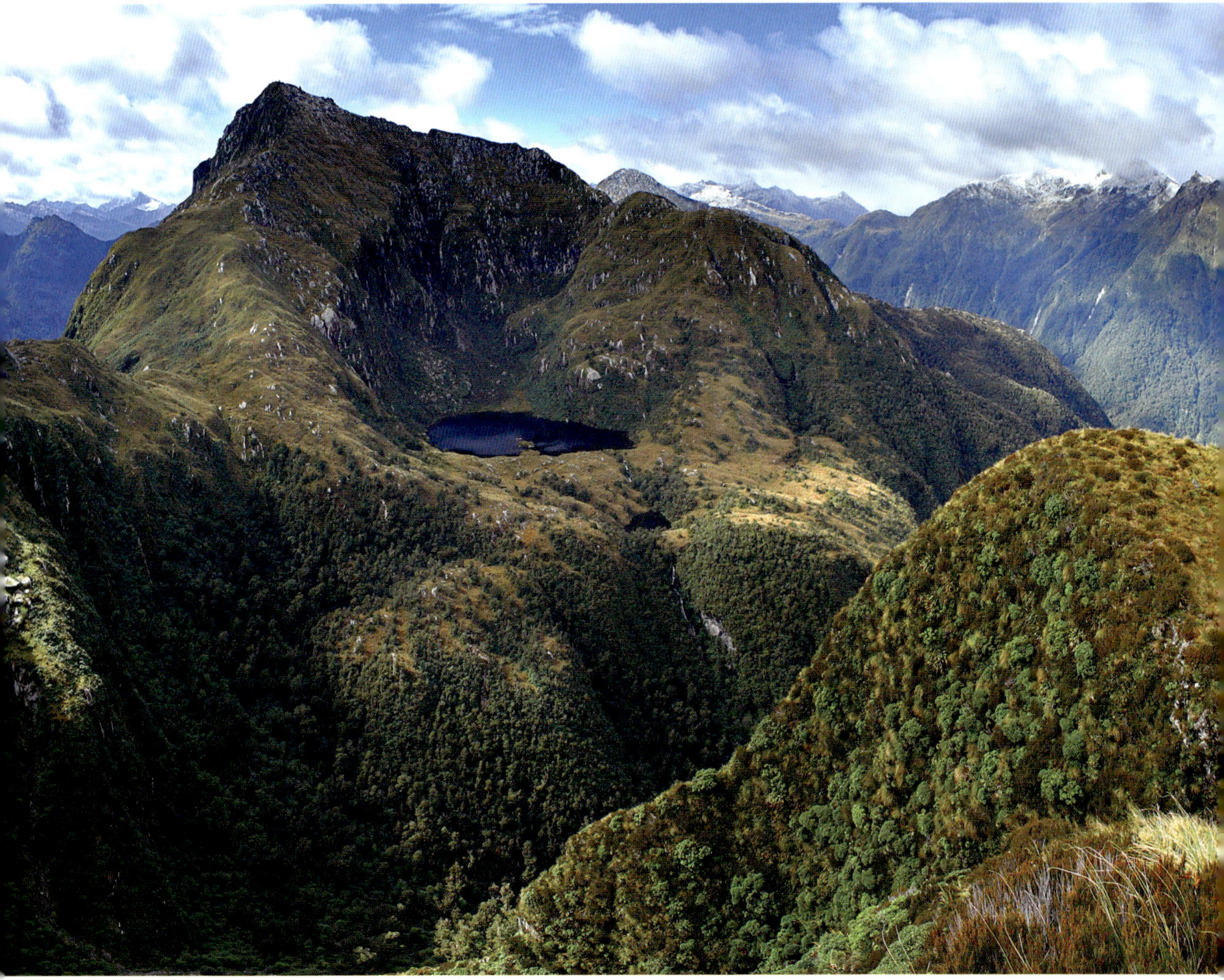

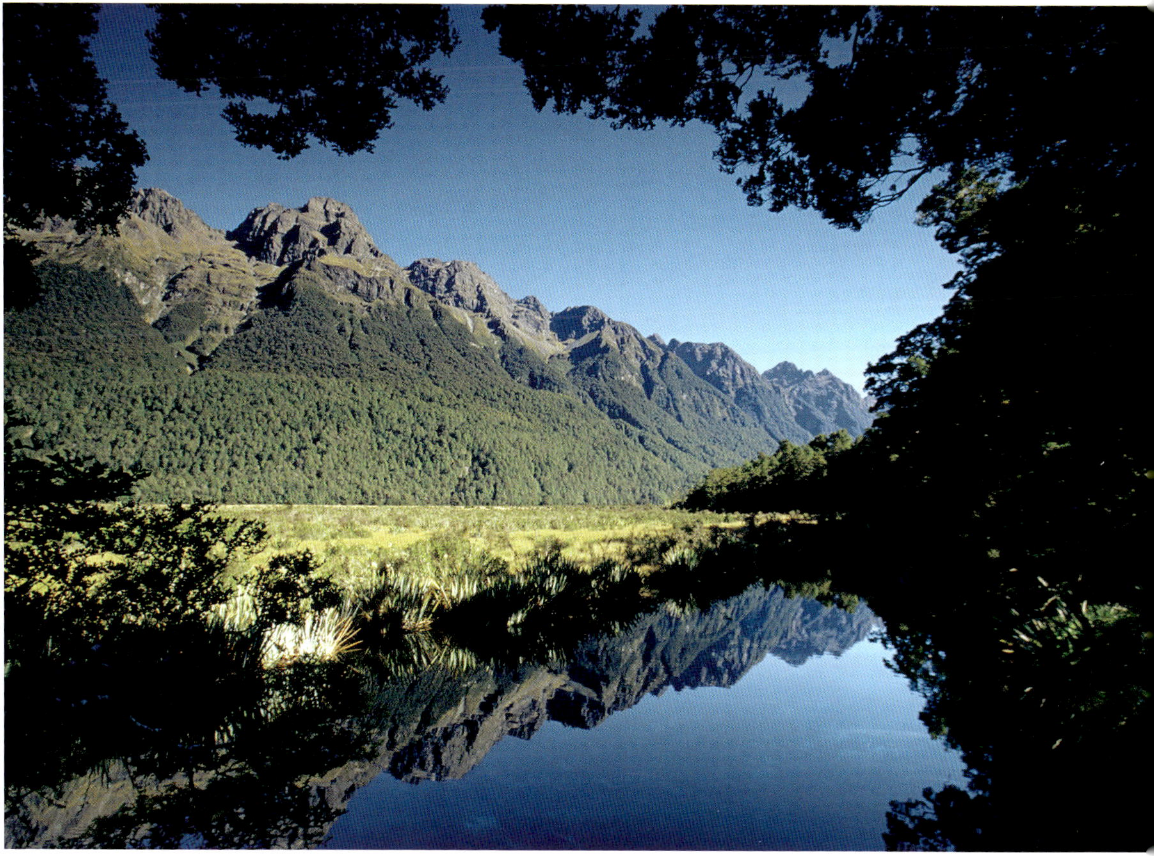

Left: Fiordland is immense, with many areas that rarely hear a human footfall. The Glaisnock Wilderness Area has been preserved in its natural wild state.

Above: Mt Eglinton, the Earl Mountains and the Mirror Lakes are among the many extraordinary sights enjoyed by travellers on the Milford Sound road.

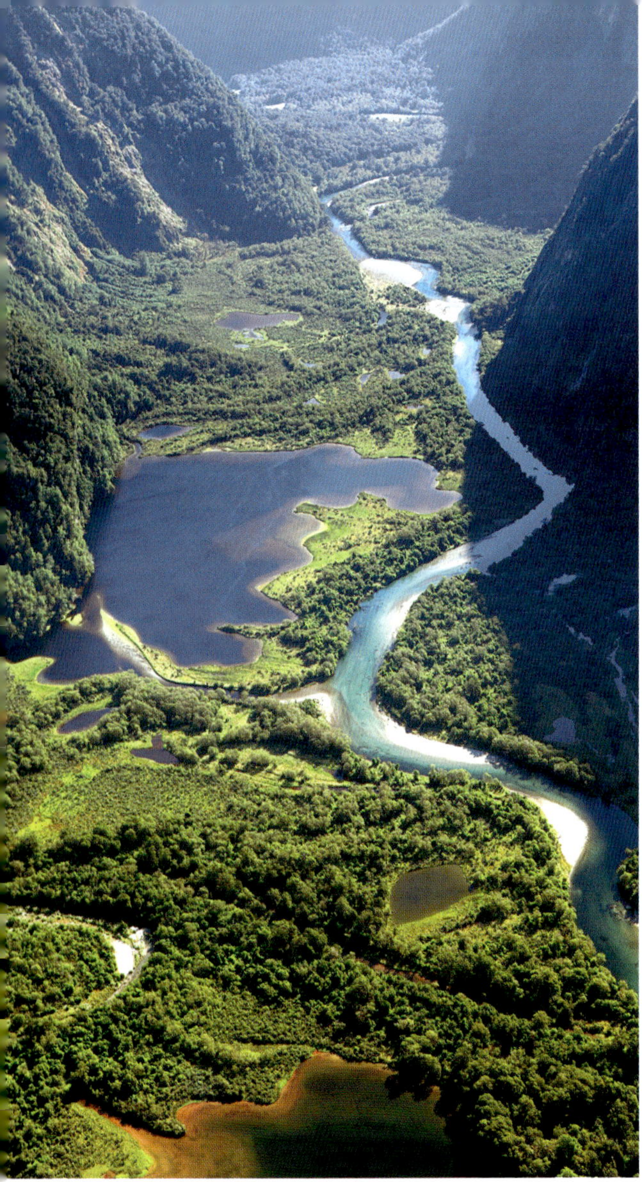

Left: On their last day on the Milford Track, hikers follow the Arthur River down a stunning U-shaped glacial valley to Milford Sound.

Below: The Kepler Track takes an exhilarating route along an alpine ridgeline before dropping down to the comfort and safety of Iris Burn Hut.

Right: Mitre Peak, its steep faces plunging deep into Milford Sound, is the classic and unforgettable image of Fiordland National Park.

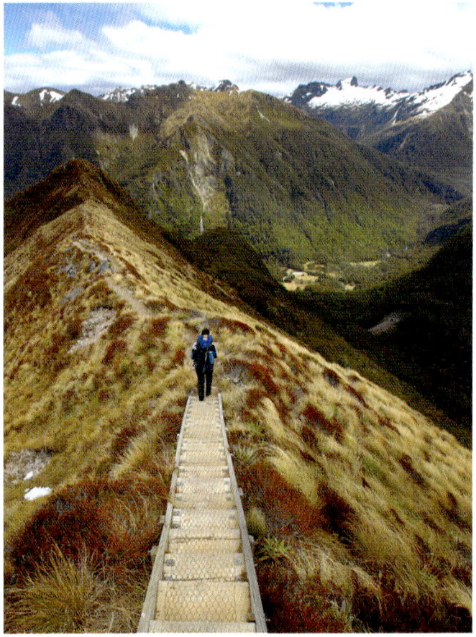

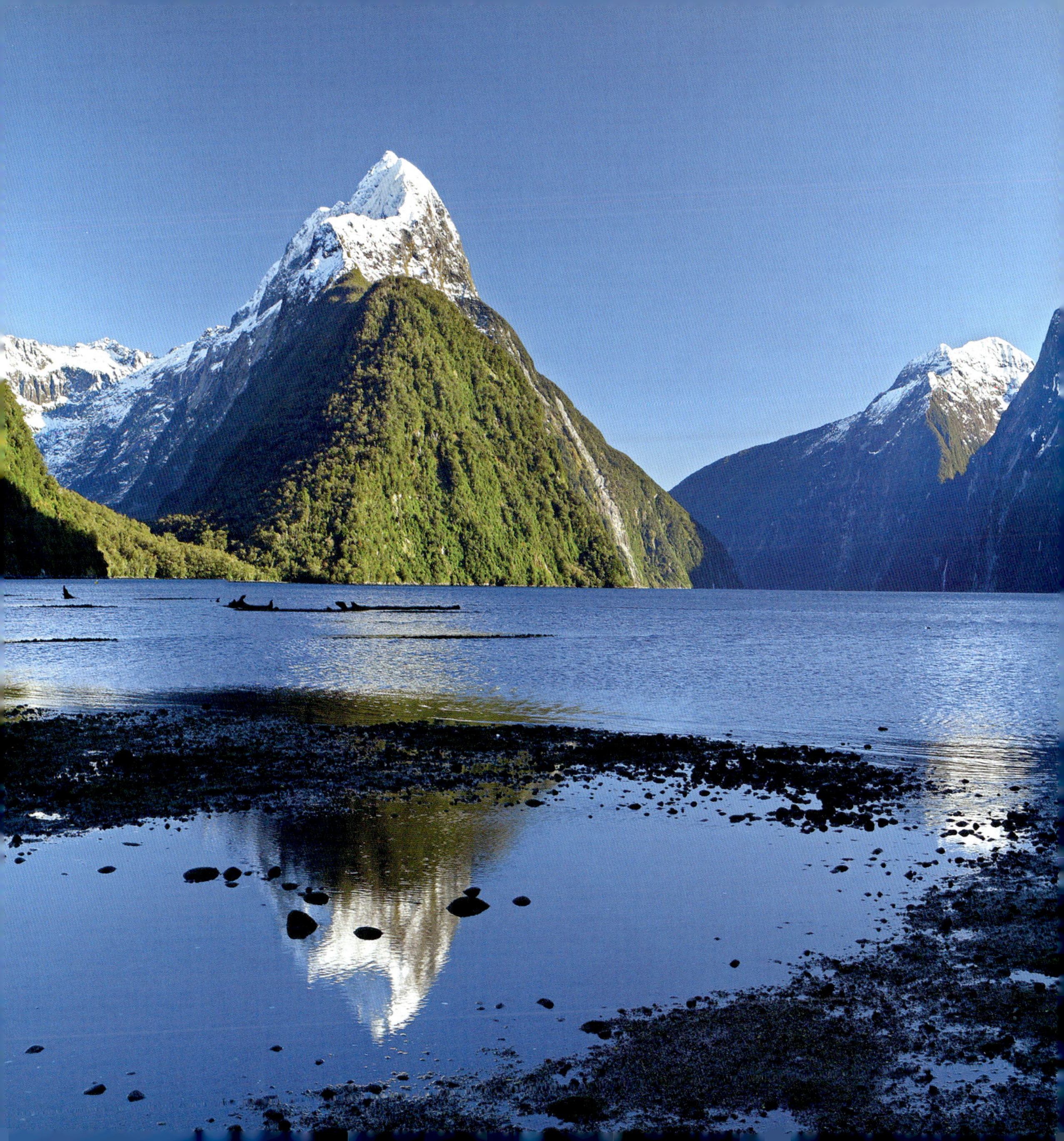

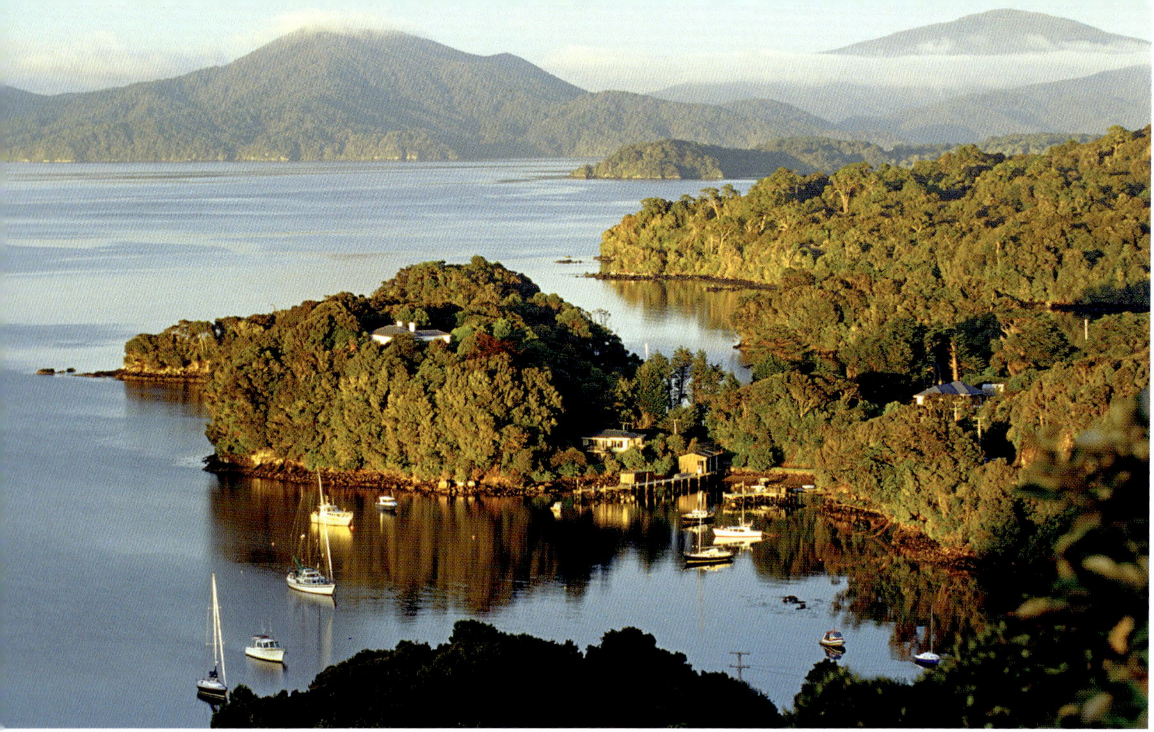

RAKIURA

Part of New Zealand, and yet apart from it, unspoiled Stewart Island/Rakiura is home to New Zealand's newest national park. More than 85 per cent of this subantarctic island, which is just a short flight or ferry ride away from the mainland, is dedicated as a park to protect the dense rainforest, rough hill country, granite domes, wetlands and picture-perfect sandy beaches and bays. Seals, penguins, owls, parrots and kiwi thrive in this sanctuary at the southernmost edge of New Zealand, as do many rare and endangered plants. The Maori name of the island, Rakiura, means 'glowing sky', a reference perhaps to the Southern Lights or the glorious sunsets often seen from this exposed and isolated spot.

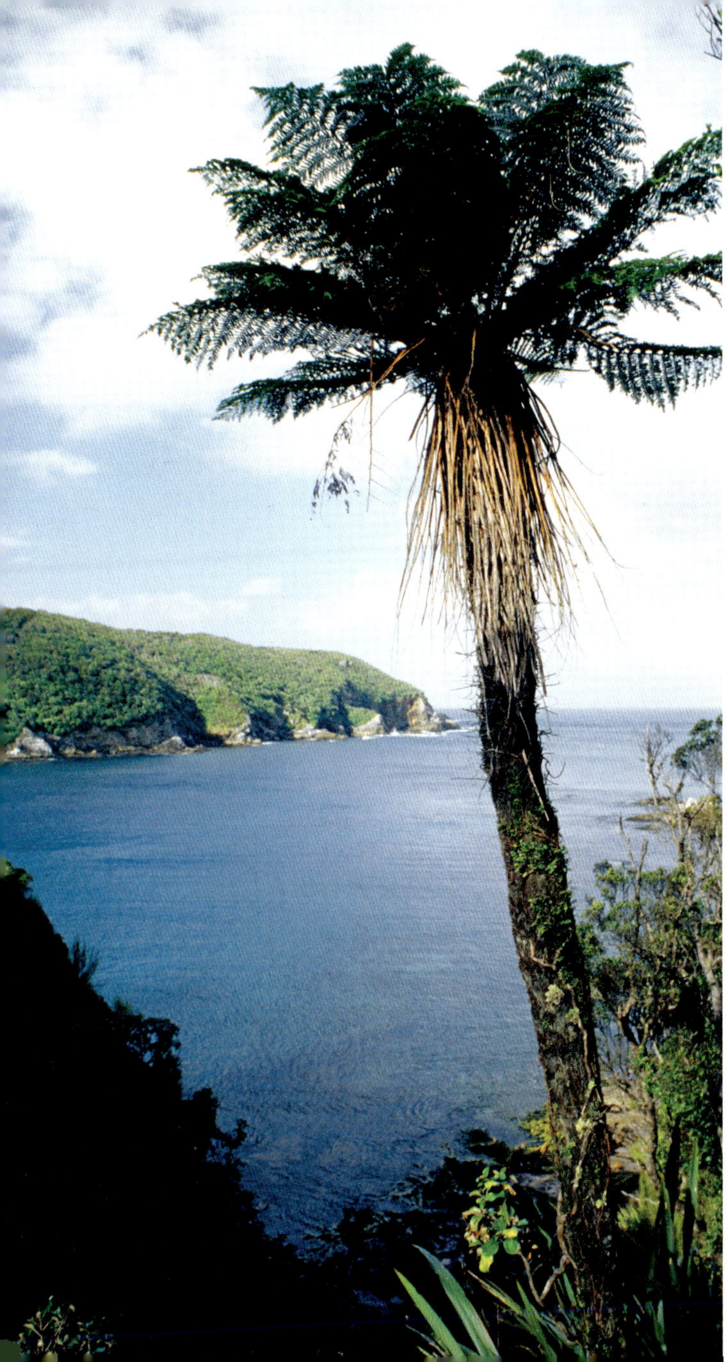

Far left: Paterson Inlet is a deep incision into the centre of Stewart Island/ Rakiura. The bays that fringe it are havens for weekenders and yachties; behind them lie the forests and hills of the national park.

Left: Katote is a feature of Rakiura's forests. It is easily distinguished from its tree fern relatives by its 'grass skirt'.

Below: Rakiura offers some of New Zealand's best bird-watching opportunities. Among the prizes for patient observers is the Stewart Island brown kiwi.

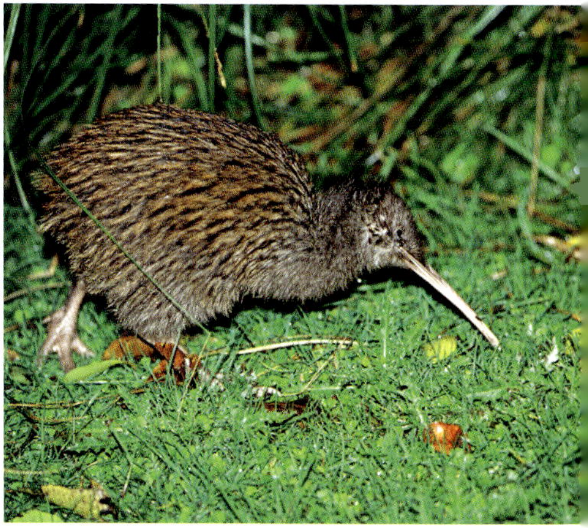

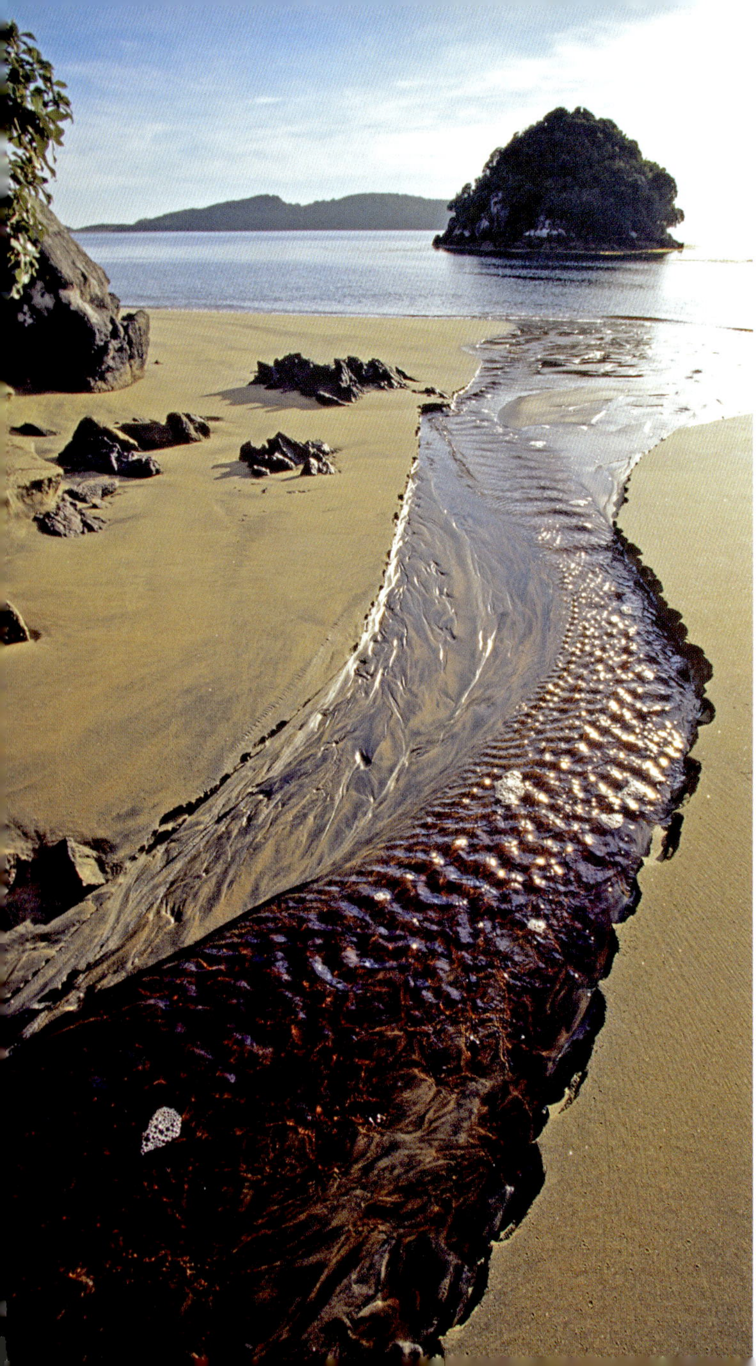

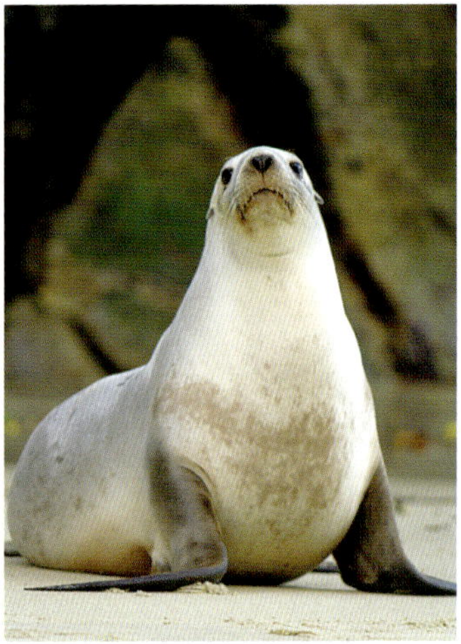

Left: Sydney Cove, Ulva Island. This island in Paterson Inlet has been cleared of predators to provide a sanctuary for rare and endangered species.

Above: The New Zealand sea lion, most common in the subantarctic islands, is also found in Rakiura National Park.

Right: Idyllic Maori Beach in Wooding Bay is a highlight for trampers on the Rakiura Track, one of New Zealand's Great Walks.

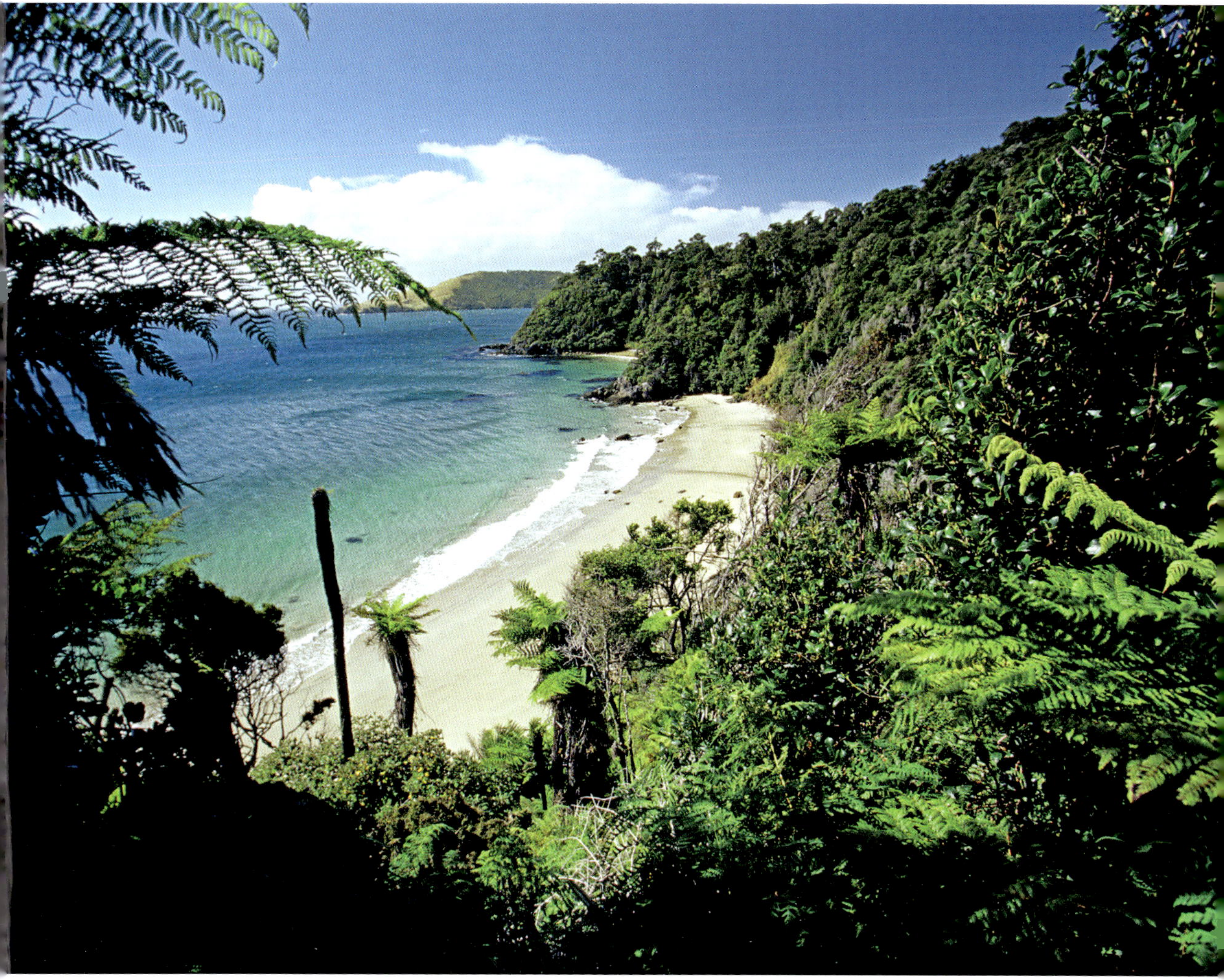

First published in 2011 by New Holland Publishers (NZ) Ltd
Auckland • Sydney • London • Cape Town

www.newhollandpublishers.co.nz

218 Lake Road, Northcote, Auckland 0627, New Zealand
Unit 1, 66 Gibbes Street, Chatswood, NSW 2067, Australia
86–88 Edgware Road, London W2 2EA, United Kingdom
80 McKenzie Street, Cape Town 8001, South Africa

ISBN: 978 1 86966 332 2

Publishing manager: Christine Thomson
Project editor: Olivia Park
Writer: Alison Dench
Editor: Matt Turner
Design: Trevor Newman

Front cover: The volcanic cone of Mt Ngauruhoe, Tongariro National Park, in winter.
Title page: The Harris, Forbes and Humboldt ranges at sunset, Mt Aspiring National Park.
Contents page: Tramper looking towards Lake Lockett, Kahurangi National Park.
Back cover: From top to bottom; Mackay Falls, Fiordland National Park; Fiordland crested penguin; Koura Beach, Kahurangi National Park.

A catalogue record for this book is available from the National Library of New Zealand.

10 9 8 7 6 5 4 3 2 1

Colour reproduction by Pica Digital Pte Ltd
Printed in China through Colorcraft Ltd, Hong Kong

Photography credits: Phil Suisted, p52 left, p57 above.